For the Love of a Dog

AMANDA BROOKFIELD is the author of fifteen published novels, including *Relative Love*, *Before I Knew You* and *The Love Child*. Her fiction has been translated into several languages. This is her first work of non-fiction. Amanda has two sons and lives in London with one cat, and a dog.

For the Love of a Dog

A memoir of meltdown, recovery,
and a Golden Doodle

Amanda Brookfield

An Anima Book

This is an Anima book, first published in the UK in 2018
by Head of Zeus Ltd

9 7 5 3 1 2 4 6 8

A catalogue record for this book is available from
the British Library.

ISBN (HB): 9781788542920
ISBN (E): 9781788542913

Typeset by Adrian McLaughlin

Printed and bound in Great Britain by
CPI Group (UK) Ltd, Croydon CR0 4YY

Head of Zeus Ltd
5–8 Hardwick Street
London EC1R 4RG

WWW.HEADOFZEUS.COM

For Amanda R

RENFREWSHIRE COUNCIL	
245721121	
Bertrams	29/10/2018
636.700	£16.99
JOH	

You will love again the stranger who was your self.
Give wine. Give bread. Give back your heart
to itself, to the stranger who has loved you
all your life, whom you ignored
for another, who knows you by heart.
Take down the love letters from the bookshelf,
the photographs, the desperate notes,
peel your own image from the mirror.
Sit. Feast on your life.

From 'Love after Love' by Derek Walcott

1

Falling Apart

A couple of years ago my mother died. She was eighty-one, grumpily frustrated with old age and not in tip-top health, but it was a terrible shock. She could still drive, but on the fateful day she was out shopping with a carer, the one she really liked (one grasps at such small mercies), when she suddenly announced she felt a bit queasy. She had a sit-down, but once they were back in the car she began to slur her words. Thanks to her quick-thinking companion, an ambulance was there in fifteen minutes, but soon after getting to hospital Mum slipped into a coma. The doctors said she had suffered a massive brain haemorrhage and didn't have long. My siblings and I, scattered round the

UK, hared down motorways and rail tracks to get to her bedside, but only my eldest sister made it in time. When I arrived Mum was still warm, just, but so utterly departed. It was my first time with a dead body. They are not so easy to hug.

A good death in many ways, therefore. There was no fear, no trauma to speak of. She had someone with her, someone who cared and knew what to do. It had been a bright, happy morning. They had been to the bank, the butcher's, the farm shop – a farewell tour, as it turned out, of all her favourite local haunts, places where she was known and talked to and made to feel at home. A good end to a good innings (the platitudes come thick and fast). If I could make an advance booking of a similarly peaceful end for myself, I would. Indeed, it was one of those endings that one might, reasonably, be tempted to call a blessing. Mum certainly would have. She had an off–on, mostly on, relationship with God and was very into blessings. But the thing about grief is it isn't logical. It blasts a hole inside you, one that heals – or not – in its own good time.

When you lose the second parent – it was twenty years since Dad's death – you lose the first all over again. Nothing had prepared me for this. They were such a devoted pair. Dad had lived on in her, through her, keeping us connected to him. Now without Mum we were, in the truest sense, orphans. And yet what luxury not to be orphaned until one's sixth decade! Talk about First World problems. I knew that. Or at least my brain did. My heart had other ideas. Losing Mum was like losing a chunk of my past, the anchor to my beginnings, the storage chest of family history, the ballast to us all.

I am not the sort of person people expect to fall apart. More to the point, I am not the sort of person *I* expect to fall apart. My life, troughs and peaks notwithstanding, has been and remains so fortunate. Health, wonderful children, solvency (I am touching wood as I type – the troughs and peaks teach caution), modest literary success, a musical ear, a panoply of fantastic friends – the list is an embarrassment of riches. Yes, loved ones have died – a couple of close friends, dear Mum of course, my sweet niece, cruelly lost when she was only five, and darling Dad, long before he was ready to go (he would never have been ready to go) – and the collapse of my marriage after twenty-six years certainly wasn't in my original game plan or something I would recommend for those seeking a stress-free existence. But I have always bounced back. That is my thing. Bouncing. Being positive. Ms Find-The-Silver-Lining, *c'est moi*.

So no one was more shocked than me when, one sunny spring day the year following Mum's death, I broke down. And I mean that quite literally: falling onto my knees, unable to breathe, howling. Even as my legs buckled I knew this was the real deal, that I was in the most major trouble of my life, that no silver linings were available, no matter how hard I rummaged in my cupboard of learned wisdom or scrutinized the horizon. The trigger was the end of a new relationship in which I had invested all my hopes. The man changed his mind. The word 'heartbreak' is so hackneyed, but on that spring day I understood it for the first time. My chest exploded, taking my brain with it.

Smithereens. Bomb fragments. The physical pain was extraordinary and impossible to imagine ever finding an end. Grieving for my mother, I had felt as if I had lost my past. Now, with this new sorrow, it was as if I had lost my future too.

It is hard not to sound melodramatic – it seems so now to the sane version of me looking back at the insane – but as I collapsed onto the floor of my study, animal sounds coming from some place I had not known I possessed, it was the fear of my despair that was almost as bad as the despair itself. To be capable of such a total lack of hope. It was terrifying. Without hope there is no point to anything. I crawled to the window and looked out. My house is tall and my study is on the first floor, with big low sash windows overlooking a stone patio.

Any novelist will tell you that even in the white heat of emotion there is an element inside that watches. We are the observers of the world, so we learn to observe ourselves. It is our job. Yet pressing my face against my study window that day, there was no part of me watching. I was too lost. I saw only the patio below the smeared glass under my fingertips. It wasn't concrete, but it was stone. Hard enough, surely, to do a decent job.

No, a stray puppy did not come romping into view from a neighbouring garden, a tail-wagging bundle of joy that made me see life was worth living after all. Art can conjure such handy twists, but Life takes a little longer to sort out. In my case, my eye-line also happened to be level with my phone, perched on the end of my desk. I am proudly unneedy – confessing to sadness has always felt tantamount to admitting to failure – but I lunged for my mobile much as a drowning person might grab at a piece of driftwood. The most recent number was my eldest sister's, so I pressed that, even though I was incapable of speech and had no expectation of an answer since I knew she was at work, hectic as always.

Somehow she answered. I was incomprehensible. Mum was always good in a crisis, and the sister has inherited the trait. Within minutes she was saying she would come to London. She commanded me to call someone to be with me until she got there. She rearranged meetings. She alerted the other sister.

The brother. Nephews and nieces were warned to rally round. The cavalry gathered. The safety net was spread out. I fell into it, flailing. Mum would have been proud of her family.

We all have a well of grief. Different events feed into it. But sometimes they merge, rise up and threaten to drown us out of being.

When I first flung out the dog idea it was more to give the appearance of thinking positively than because I truly was. The saintly cohort who had closed protectively around me in the days and weeks following my meltdown, reacted encouragingly. The poor loves dared not do anything else, for I fear the despair was impossible to hide. I could have said I was thinking of getting a pet cobra and they would have grinned and said 'splendid' and started making suggestions as to where to buy live vermin and the best place to park its cage.

Lurking behind their sweetness, however, was an understandable, gently expressed scepticism. As things stood I was clearly in no fit state to look after myself, let alone a dog. In addition to the usual catalogue of misery symptoms – constant weeping, inability to sleep, disinclination to eat – I had grown clumsy and careless about everyday things like walking through doors and turning corners. The bruises on my arms and legs were impressive, though easy to hide, thank goodness. Even my reclusive cat, Tiger Lily, had grown warier than usual, sensing some mysterious new order of play that required a greater level of avoidance. Once, during the early, dire days, I managed to slice my hand open while attempting to wash up a knife. I remember watching the blood spout into the washing-up water thinking, well yes, that's fine, let's just see where this goes. Luckily the member of the family with me that day (they visited in shifts) took a more proactive view.

My zombie state notwithstanding, no one would argue that I have ever been an obvious candidate for canine ownership. There are myriad reasons for this, the most obvious being that I hate mornings. Dawn starts, the rack of the school run (having to be organized while still half asleep), were for me by far the hardest aspects of early motherhood. One of the greatest pleasures of regaining my independence during the last decade has been the development of a contrastingly slow morning ritual: tea, papers, a hot bath, porridge with a smidge of Radio 4, a whizz through the Super Fiendish sudoku to get my brain in gear before sitting down to work. People choosing to pull on wellies in the chill damp of first light in order to release their dogs to the pleasures of peeing, pooing and chasing balls have always evoked in me a sort of baffled pity. Even visiting my parents, who became owners to a string of memorable hounds during their latter years, I was happy for the pretext to go on a walk in the countryside, but only ever in the afternoons, and only then if I was in the right mood.

The foremost reason for my unsuitability as a dog owner, however, is that I am a novelist. My life is indoorsy to the highest degree. For thirty years my default position has been sitting at my desk trying to write. Even more crucially, I am a *reluctant* novelist, never happier than when given the chance to escape the bonds of my vocation and plunge into society: lunches, dinners, teas, cinemas, theatres, art galleries – I would go to the opening of a flea circus if invited. Getting divorced and waving off my adult children had only encouraged such proclivities. The ungenerous might say that had turned me into a gadabout. I would humbly counter that after three decades of being padlocked to deadlines and word counts, one has to leap at every slim opportunity to get out into the world. A writer has to live life as well as write about it.

But the meltdown meant I couldn't write anyway. I couldn't even read. Deep upset shreds one's powers of concentration as well as one's confidence. The last thing I wanted was to plunge into society. I kept some of the unavoidable commitments in those early weeks and shudder to recall them: weeping volubly in public spaces – trains, streets, restaurants – grief knows no shame. Friends were so patient, so kind. Yet staying home alone with the cat was just as bad. The most basic domestic tasks had become mountainous challenges. Halfway through changing the sheets, writing a shopping list or loading the dishwasher, I would freeze, unable to go on, seeing only the futility of everything. A change was called for. Something drastic.

'One of the smaller breeds then?' ventured the elder sister. All my siblings live in the country. Both sisters have dogs of their own, quite large ones. They also have things like veg patches. I am the Townie.

I am scrolling through dog-buying websites. The puppy talk has expanded over the weeks, for me still a handy façade of forward-thinking where there was none. Besides which, googling puppies makes you feel fuzzy inside – a scientifically proven fact, since we apparently release oxytocin, the bonding chemical, just from watching them play roly-poly. 'A dog should be dog-sized, don't you think?' I say absently. 'Small ones are silly.'

'What about a rescue one instead then? They are supposed to be the most loving. They're so grateful to be taken in. Have you googled Battersea? Think of all the dogs desperate for a good home. And they always take them back if it doesn't work out.'

Battersea. A creature who had suffered, who

needed extra love, extra care. I simply wasn't up to it. I felt found out. The superficiality of my interest was laid bare. I just liked the idea of a puppy. I was never going to act on it. I was a coward and a fraud. 'Well, a puppy would be more fun, you have to admit.'

'It would certainly keep you busy, that's for sure. But it's entirely up to you.' The sister gives me a beady-eyed look. She could see through me. Everybody could. They were all humouring the dog chat because they assumed it would pass. As did I. The younger son, who had waged a twenty-year campaign for a dog during his formative years and finally given up, started sending me links to things like Great Danes, Pyrenean mountain dogs and St Bernards. He knew I was never going to get one of those. It was just a game. Something To Cheer Mum Up. A game they all played, with such earnestness and energy, such devotion, that sometimes it only added fuel to my tears. Kindness has always had a tendency to knock me flying.

★

Conversation is like wildfire. You mention something, an interest in Barcelona, say, or puppies, and people start telling you about Spanish aunts and dog breeders. As the weeks passed I found myself taking down website addresses, telephone numbers, names of dog owners. The loyal cohort had lives to return to. There was talk of counselling but I didn't want that. One of the sisters is a counsellor anyway and she was working her magic with me, calling every day, picking up no matter when I rang, making me feel that she had absolutely nothing in her life (a family of six, full-time job, house-moving, a dog!) to attend to except the need to hear her younger sister sobbing down the phone, going round in circles about her shattered state. Falling apart is, above all things, so very dull. One is stuck on a wheel: monotonous, repetitious, selfish.

One hot Saturday in early summer I found myself on a train to Wales. It was good to have something to do, somewhere to be. A train to Wales. The fact that I had an appointment with a place that bred a mesmerizing selection of fashionable cross-breed dogs felt almost incidental. One of my scribbled recommendations had led to a website, which had led to a phone call, which had led to this date. I had kept meaning to cancel. Or at least postpone. But somehow I never did. On the phone making the original appointment, I had feigned certainty, declaring a specific interest in cockapoos. In truth I simply liked the name, and a friend had sent me a picture of hers which looked cute. Not too big. Not too small. Not too hairy. Fun and friendly. Such was the depth of my research.

On the train I started reading Somerset Maugham's *Mrs Craddock* and found myself so engrossed I began to dread the arrival of my stop. I knew this was good. It had been several months since I was able to lose myself in a story, months, in other words, since I had been able to concentrate on anything beyond the sorry events of my own life. Mrs Craddock cannot find love and endures many travails, yet her mundane journey is rich and interesting, a life worth living. Maugham's masterful, tender, acutely observed tale wrapped itself around my heart. It made me feel less alone, more understood. That is what all the best books do. It is what I strive, however imperfectly, to give my own readers.

I trudged to the taxi rank outside Newport station. It was drizzling and I was dressed for high summer. The last thing I was in the mood for was a long ride into the middle of the Welsh countryside to talk about dogs. I knew I should have driven myself from London, but I hadn't felt up to it. Car journeys are hard if you are feeling fragile: too many road signs, too much headspace for internal negative voice-overs. The taxi driver was chirpy but soon grew subdued as we ploughed ever deeper into the verdure of Wales, following his satnav instructions over humpback bridges and down a maze of narrow windy lanes to a place that, literally, appeared not to exist. On some level this made perfect sense to me. My mission wasn't about the mission itself. I was simply seeking respite from being home alone. Filling another empty day. Going through motions.

I had a phone number for the dog-breeding place, but it took a lot more driving to find a spot with a strong enough signal to use it. Satnavs always took people the wrong way, I was merrily informed during the course of the intricate instructions for arrival that ensued, though quite how or why this was the case I was never able to ascertain. When we finally arrived, my driver cheered up immensely at the sight of my thirty-five pounds and what he clearly perceived as the astonishing request to return in an hour's time to undertake the same journey in reverse. I was merely grateful that I had thought to go to a cash machine at Waterloo station. I didn't care about the money. All I wanted was for this masquerade of a day to be done with, to be free to scuttle back the way I had come.

I was shown into a small interview room: a desk with two chairs, the walls studded with posters of happy hounds and charts about canine health. My interviewer, a young woman with soft brown eyes and a soothingly lyrical Welsh accent, asked me to tell her what I was looking for in a dog. Oh lord. I chattered on about working at home and the friend with the nice cockapoo. When I had finished she paused, sucked her pen and asked if I had given any thought to a Golden Doodle. They were more chilled out, she said, which might work well with my writing.

It turned out you don't get to meet any puppies until much deeper into the process. Instead I was shown into a dog playground area and introduced to several fine but intimidatingly ebullient fully grown animals. The cockapoos were the nuttiest of all. Hyper. Demanding. My strained nerves twanged. A dog would ruin my life. I couldn't look after one of these. I couldn't look after myself. I was in the middle of Wales making a tit of myself.

The last of my introductions was to a Golden Doodle called India. She had an off-white, short, curly coat and was the only creature calm to the point of indifference. She liked the girl in charge of her but had no interest in me. I was relieved. I had followed through on a recommendation. I had conducted further research into what was plainly a mad idea. In the process I had rediscovered the joy of reading. I could bow out gracefully. Get back to *Mrs Craddock*. Get home. Another long day done with.

Back in the interview room it transpired that tests that very morning had confirmed India was expecting puppies. She had been crossed with a small poodle called Claude, my sweet-voiced interviewer explained. The litter wouldn't be due for three months, and not ready for collection until the autumn. If I was interested, my name could go on a list. There was a small refundable deposit to pay. Cancellation was possible at any time. It just meant my name would be on a list. Nearer the time, I could return and meet both parents properly, if I was still interested. Before eventually meeting the puppies. Eight weeks after they were born. Once they had been medically checked. To choose one. If I was still interested.

I'd like to be able to say that, sitting at that table that Saturday afternoon, deciding to Keep All Options Open was a rational tactic undertaken by a rational person. In fact it was pure indecision that made me reach for my chequebook. The following day felt a world away, let alone the autumn. And the deposit, though significant, was refundable*. Through the window I could see my taxi had arrived, ready for our return safari through the countryside.

'We'll call you when the puppies are born,' the girl said as I signed the cheque. 'You can decide then.'

A few months after my father died I had the most extraordinary dream. I walked into a room and there he was, bending over his desk. He looked up and smiled, and a blaze of happiness coursed through me. The smile was so radiant, and real to the finest detail: his thin mouth, the small gaps in his nicotine-stained teeth, his blue eyes twinkling through the thick lenses of his specs.

'Hello, Small,' he said.

Some part of me knew it was a dream, but I

---

* Those hoping for an actual costing on the price of a Golden Doodle puppy will have to look elsewhere. SWAT kidnap teams might helicopter into my garden to steal my dog away were I to divulge what I paid for her. Note to self: there is no price tag on happiness.

ached to touch him, to be held. I moved closer and he turned to greet me, opening his arms. Some inner core of me braced itself. I knew he wasn't real. I knew he was dead. I stepped into the circle of the embrace expecting to feel nothing but air, that missed-step feeling when a foot reaches for a stair that isn't there. But the opposite happened. The father-strength of him closed round me, as solid, as real, as a tree. I could feel every sinew of him, of his love. I woke weeping, flooded with joy.

I wanted to dream of my mother, but nothing came. Only images of the man I had lost lapped inside my head. I fought them back. I did not want to dream of him. I had done enough of that already. Love is action, and he had walked away.

2

Slippery Slopes

On the day Mabel wriggled her way into the world, I was in Rome on a minibreak with a sister, one of several sibling-plots to get me through the year without toppling back into my abyss. Puppies were far from my mind. The city gleamed and steamed in the July heat. Rome, for the record, and much to my amazement, is as mind-blowing as it is cracked up to be. Round every bend a fresh piece of antique magnificence waits to cosh you over the head: towering temples, rippling statues of gods and beasts and men, the broken cloistered majesty of the Coliseum, not to mention the epic architecture and glories contained in the papal city. It is like being on a film set. But infinitely better because it is real. The sister and I gasped and gawped, humbled by the sheer scale of human endeavour on all sides. Humans try so hard; that's what struck me most. They – we – build hopes and civilizations, watch them get knocked down, then try to build them up again. The striving is all.

The heat sapped our strength. To survive we fell in and out of fan-cooled cafés, recharging ourselves with cold beers and plates of fresh pasta. For the first time in months I began to know real hunger, real thirst, real fatigue. We laughed. A lot. One day, trapped on a tourist bus circling the city (long story), we got the giggles in the way that used to happen when we were kids. Loud, hysterically out of control, we were briefly and, much to our helpless embarrassment, of more interest to our fellow passengers than the passing monuments of classical antiquity. It took a good thirty minutes to get ourselves under control, and then only by resolutely not looking at each other. I felt a stab of wild happiness just to know such a capacity for joy was still inside me, that I wasn't a husk after all.

By the Spanish Steps we found the unprepossessing house in which John Keats, mightiest and youngest of the Romantic poets, had drawn his final, agonizing consumptive breaths two hundred years before. My sister hovered out of sight while I paid homage to my hero in the stuffy box of a bedroom. I did not need to ask for this. She just sensed the private import of my pilgrimage and tactfully granted me the space in which to savour it.

Love is knowing someone and being known. I had said this to the man who had left. Now, in the aching emptiness of his absence, I saw that it was my closest family who were proving the truth of the observation. Day in and day out since my meltdown they had been reading me, understanding me, listening to me. Carrying me. All this when, behind the scenes, we were in fact starting to face excruciating family trouble thanks to the vagueness of our mother's will. Mum had meant well, we knew. She had always had a thing about treating the four of us fairly. The open nature of her last testament was simply a reflection of that; the inability, in other words, to make choices that

she feared might be deemed 'unfair'. Without such
explicit guidance, however, fissures had been opening up between us, as fissures do when lawyers are
involved and money is at stake.

But in Rome it was as if none of that trouble
existed. The sister and I talked of Mum solely in the
context of missing her and because she had loved
Italy and its troves of classical and Renaissance
treasures. We recalled guiltily how she had urged
us to visit this very city and the little heed we had
paid. Somewhere among the scores of collapsing
family albums and ancient photo slides (still to be
sorted, along with everything else, because of the
ongoing problems) were all the pictures she had
taken of the very things that we were now gaz-
ing upon in awe. In her prime she had been an
intrepid photographer (back when it was not the
easy hobby it is today) but we had largely ignored
that too. Talking of such things as we explored,
marvelled and roasted under blazing Roman skies,
Mum started to edge back into focus; not as the
endearing maddening old lady she had become,
racking us all with worry, nor as the owner of a

legacy causing us such dissension, but as the multi-faceted and remarkable woman who had loved our father and all four of us to the core.

There were dogs galore in Rome. Skulking, flea-ridden strays. Pooches hanging out of arms and handbags like the accessories they are, and more traditional pets, dawdling on short leads among the endless throngs of hot legs. God, how I pitied them. Cooped up on that burning summer stage, their tongues pink and lolling with the effort to stay cool; no space for delicious doggy madness, no space indeed to be their true animal selves. Mabel (newly born, as yet unowned, unnamed) crossed my mind then all right, but only as an abstraction, a bullet dodged. A city dweller myself, I saw afresh the selfish madness of my puppy schemes and planned to scotch them as soon as I got home.

A change of geography can only do so much. The inner life travels with us. At the sight of my empty

London house, I could feel the old tightness clamping round my heart. Here was my home-alone life, waiting to swallow me up. Closing the front door, I wept. Yet more weeping. I blush to recall it. With hindsight I would say that years of tears were pouring out. I had been such a stubbornly sunny creature, bouncing her way through divorce and death and loss. But like water, unhappiness will eventually find a way to surface. Somehow. Whether we like it or not. It pushes through the cracks, widening them before they can be closed.

Cats are designed differently to dogs. They are takers not givers, granting the favour of affection on their own terms. Already insulted by five days of abandonment, Tiger Lily greeted my sobbing re-entrance into her world with barely concealed disdain. While I trudged round opening windows, flicking dead flies off the sills and ramming clothes into the washing machine, she stalked me from doorways, tail high with indignation, glaring. She wanted food, not love (although her barrel tummy, the product of over-eagerness by the cat feeder, told me it was the least of her requirements). When I gave her some anyway she guzzled it down and then took herself off to the back of her favourite armchair, settling into her chicken-ready-to-roast position, back towards me. A Keep Out sign could not have been clearer. There would be some relenting, I knew. In a day or two. Occasional leg-brushing would be reintroduced, along with a daily five-minute ration of close morning attention while I lay in bed attempting to drink my first mug of tea. The newspaper would be head-butted out of the way to make room for some intense chest massage (claws out) and a couple of nose nuzzles. Then she would be off to one of her secret hiding places till tea time. On her own terms, like I say.

Don't get me wrong, I love Tiger Lily. More importantly, after ten years' acquaintance, I respect her. She has issues, as who wouldn't after being abandoned in the street at two weeks old. She had known no nurturing during the time when it mattered most. That she has learned to trust me in spite of this brutal genesis is something I treasure. When she puts the Keep Out sign up it is always for good reason. Wanting more from her, as I did after Rome, felt like my failure, not hers. Nonetheless, I could feel the dog-desire creeping back in. A dog would never be so standoffish. A dog would smother me in licks. A dog would go bonkers with joy if I had been away. Yet that is precisely why Tiger Lily would freak out. A puppy would be a nuclear bomb in her already precarious world. At best she would have a nervous breakdown. At worst she would leave.

I relish solitude, as every writer must. Books don't get written without it. But loneliness is different to solitude. It pounds away inside you, worse than the worst toothache. Its silence is like a road drill. After Rome it was as bad as it has ever been. My finished novel needed revision, but the effort of attending to it was Herculean. Alone at my desk, my head buzzed with the white noise of doubt, of self-criticism. The story I had written felt remote, the work of someone else, someone who didn't matter. You need certainty when you are writing. The confidence to make decisions, to put one foot in front of the other. A lot like life, really. And I had lost all mine.

It was C.S. Lewis who said that grief is a sort of fear, and at last I understood exactly what he meant. That hollowness of missing someone – whether it be a deserting lover, a dead parent, or both – is so very similar to a state of being afraid. The terror is all the worse for being as vague as it is prevalent: a constant, panicking sense of not knowing quite what to do, of watching oneself falter, of having no idea how to regain personal purpose. Out in the world, talking to people, doing things with people, I was managing. But it was all an act. Alone, I was still completely at sea.

A week after my return from Rome, I am at my desk losing the daily battle with my manuscript, when there is a phone call from Wales. It takes me a couple of seconds to place the cosy singsong voice. 'I'm ringing to tell you that all went well. Nine pups – six boys and three girls. We can now arrange a date for you to come and choose. In six weeks' time. If you're still interested?'

Tiger Lily is draped across the chair next to my

desk. I turn my back on her. Two can play the Keep Out game. 'Oh yes, I am still interested.'

'It was a bitch you wanted, wasn't it?'

Was it? (I don't like the word 'bitch'. Too many connotations. Funny how words get like that. Layered with meanings, such bad ones sometimes that they have to be outlawed. Testimony, should one need it, to their power.) A girl dog – a bitch – would mean periods, it occurs to me suddenly. Menstruation. How did that work? How did people manage? Mops? Pads? And when she was on heat would hordes of male dogs storm my rickety-fenced garden? Would she be gang-raped in the park? My son had gleefully told me of a friend's retriever who had apparently never fully recovered from just such an incident. I might end up with an emotional wreck of a dog as well as a wreck of a cat. Not to mention their wreck of an owner.

Yet did I want a male dog if it was capable of such gross brute behaviour? They also humped chair legs and human shins. They spread their legs and licked their genitals. My peaceful TV dinners would never be the same again.

'Yes, a bitch.' The certainty in my voice gives me palpitations. Menstruation was at least something of which I had some experience, though happily not the gang rape thing.

'Lovely. In that case let's make a date for you to come and choose your puppy.'

My puppy.

'With a view to collection in early September.'

'If I don't change my mind.' I laugh, a little wildly.

My interlocutor remains professionally deadpan. 'Of course. Though please be aware that if you pull out after making your selection you will forfeit your deposit.'

Relief fuses with excitement as I jot the dates down. The doggy bullet is still zigzagging in my general direction. Decidedly dodgeable. The deposit suddenly seems a measly amount to lose. In the meantime I have two more diversionary minibreaks to enjoy – Derbyshire with the other sister, Portugal with a girlfriend. Plenty of time, still, to decide finally. I instruct myself to extract every last drop of pleasure from these indulgences. Soon I could be stuck at home with a yapping ball and chain.

*

If only there were some kind of guarantee of getting a 'nice' dog. As with people, dogs are a jumble of good and bad. You never know what might emerge, no matter how well-intentioned the dog owner. I recall one of my mother's hounds, a perfectly amiable creature, who suddenly decided – after four years – to sink its teeth into a visiting grandchild's forearm. The grandchild was two, and the dog, as my mother liked to point out when relating the tale, was in no hurry to remove its teeth. She grabbed the creature and yelled at it, but it took a while to open its jaws. It had crossed some sort of Rubicon. It liked the taste of the arm. The animal in it had triumphed. Mum loved that dog and it loved her, but she knew it had to go. The breeders kindly agreed to take it back. She wept the entire way.

I was sufficiently aware of my fragile state to be afraid of what getting a 'bad' – or even a difficult – dog might do to me. I needed a lovely loving mutt. I needed to 'succeed' at dog ownership. Otherwise, instead of keeping the abyss at bay, I knew it just might hasten its return.

Seeking reassurance, I started to share my puppy plans with a wider circle of friends. Almost without exception, the response was negative, albeit well-meaning. They knew my gadabout ways. Or thought they did. One wrote:

Dear Amanda,

Freedom is much better than a dog – it's not even close. Don't get a dog. For years our kids wanted a dog – particularly the girls – but we would always have had difficulties going away, and not having difficulties going away was more important than having a dog. Also, I knew that I'd end up walking and feeding and cleaning up after him/her. When our youngest used to plead why couldn't we have a pet, I'd tell her we already have one. She'd ask who, and I'd tell her, 'You'. She was as close as we got to having a pet.

I fired back a pithy, defensive reply along the lines of 'freedom' not being the straightforward liberating concept it is made out to be, pointing out that having some self-imposed boundaries in our lives is often what makes us effective and efficient human beings. (In my head I was thinking about the hateful power of deadlines. My novel, the first I had written for myself rather than to a contract, was at last fully revised and with my agent. It had taken three long years. Back in the day, with small children and only a few hours to myself each week, I had somehow produced a book a year, for seven years.)

My correspondent remained undeterred:

You still shouldn't get a dog. No one will want to look after it when you want to go away even if they say they'll do it.

And a 'Golden Doodle' is all wrong anyway. The name speaks for itself. It's an embarrassment masquerading as a dog. What kind of hair will it have? It'll have a haircut resembling topiary from a Capability Brown landscape, but simultaneously be a skunk-hunting enthusiast. It'll be big yet yappy, with those sharp pointy poodle teeth, and it'll take up the whole couch; you'll always be squeezed into a corner. You say the main worry is how your cat will feel. Your cat will feel embarrassed for you.

Not to put a damper on your plans.

Like I say, friends were pretty negative.

Walking in Derbyshire, it is a relief to suffer my first genuine stabs of dog envy. There are so many mutts scrambling around after their owners, livening up the landscape and the picnics, chasing sticks and jumping into streams. I want one!

Back home the date of the next trip to Wales glares out from my desk diary, getting inexorably closer. *CHOOSE PUPPY!!!* Red felt-tip capital letters and punctuation marks exclaim their author's terror.

Portugal is hot, hedonistic. Mostly I eat and sleep. I try not to think about dogs.

And then, quietly, like so many momentous things, the day arrives. Uncancelled, it feels like, rather than actively embraced, just like the entire quest. A dear animal-mad schoolfriend kindly offers to come with me. Under her command the Welsh safari is swift and fun, her excitement on my behalf infectious. First we are taken to meet the parents, Claude and India, reinforcing the fact that this is a professional process. An arranged coupling. Arranged babies. Adoption. A business. India is exactly as I remember her, middling-sized (think small lab) with a short, light toffee-coloured coat, and though friendly enough, still mostly interested in her treats and her handler. Claude, a small poodle with a neat fuzz of grey-white hair, is cool and handsome. He says his hellos between taking up poses, as if he knows he is being sized up and is trying to put on a good show. I am distracted by this stage, wanting only to cut to the chase – TO MEET THE PUPPIES – even if I decide I don't want one. Happily my companion is far more clued up and in less of a hurry. She fires off strings of vital questions about breeding lines, litters, vaccinations and medical check-ups before she is satisfied and we are finally led inside.

I defy anyone, let alone a lonely novelist with a sore heart, to sit in a puppy pen being nibbled and crawled over by three six-week-old Golden Doodles without fighting the strong urge to pop one in a pocket for keeps. For some misguided and mystifying reason (jollity? overexcitement? nerves?) I elected to wear pink trousers and a pink T-shirt that day. Think over-exuberant flamingo. Or mulched salmon. With sunburn (Portugal). It was sufficiently odd for the friend who kindly accompanied me to remark on it, but happily still not enough to ruin the snaps and film footage she then very sweetly takes with my phone. The puppies steal the show; OF COURSE the puppies steal the show! They are captivating: busy mini-mini toddlers, tumbling, burrowing, rolling. All is play. Their too-long ears are silky and their crinkly fur the colour of apricots and cream. Mabel (as yet unchosen) is the creamiest of all, near-white, in fact, compared to her sisters. Her ears are a lighter colour too, only going dark apricot at the tips. She is by far the chubbiest and also the clumsiest, with paws like snowshoes.

I pick each puppy up in turn, cooing nonsense

as they wiggle and paddle in my hands. They are soft and warm and smell faintly milky and doggy-clean. When I put them down they tumble back to continue their games, tripping over each other like drunks. Only Mabel (as yet unchosen) seems marginally happier to hang out with me. When I stroke her I can tell she likes it. After a few moments she rolls onto her back, inviting me to tickle her tummy.

And that's all it takes. The choice, suddenly, is made. Job done. A life decision in a few instants. On such pinheads do our paths turn. In addition to wanting me to stroke her tum, Mabel (now chosen, but still unnamed) is quite simply the cutest living creature I have ever seen, let alone touched. She is toy-like in her perfection. Her nose is as cold as a sea-pebble and jet black. Her eyes are molten chocolate, glinting with hope and mischief. Most of her tummy is still bare and very pink, so vulnerable that I want to bubble-wrap it – and the rest of her – to keep her safe. While her sisters try to chew my pink trousers (who can blame them?), Mabel licks my skin. Yeah, yeah, she likes the saltiness, but it doesn't feel like that. It feels like she wants me to choose her too.

A new abyss that day, then. A good one. Mabel and I falling into it together. And for those who cringe at the sentimentality of such an assertion, let me point out that it really doesn't matter if there is any truth to it. A six-week-old puppy can know virtually nothing of its feelings. And I am a sad-at-heart middle-aged woman looking for a thread of joy in a life that has turned grey. But sometimes the believing in something is all that matters, all that it takes to make it real.

3

Early Days

Two weeks remain until puppy-collection day. I have signed up the youngest son to take some time out of his busy life to join me when it comes to the seven-hour round trip. He cannot believe I am getting a dog. Neither can I. I get my garden fencing reinforced. I move Tiger Lily's base camp out of the kitchen and into a quieter room, where I install a new cat-flap into the garden. Tiger Lily does not like the flap. I have to coax her into using it with scraps of irresistible fattening food. Still she sulks, so I buy an expensive plug-in something-or-other that supposedly gives off relaxing aromas, detectable only to cats. Tiger Lily does seem a tad happier, but I could not swear to it, and this troubles me more than it should. Confidence in my own judgement is still on walkabout over the most trivial things. What to wear. When to eat. Reasons to get out of bed in the morning. Whether it is madness to get a dog. Whether it is dumb to spend twenty-five pounds on a plug-in for my cat. The guy ropes of my life are still flapping.

In latter years my mother found it hard to relax, to be happy. She agonized over the smallest decisions. One event in the diary a week was enough to send her into a flat spin. 'It's pandemonium here,' she'd say on the phone, if a dental appointment loomed or her cleaner was ten minutes late. Change distressed her. People coming and going distressed her. Being alone distressed her. I was good at cajoling her out of such anxieties – we each had our strengths when dealing with Mum – but inside my impatience would bubble. She worried about things that DID NOT MATTER. And all the cheering-up never lasted. The clouds regrouped, in minutes sometimes, darkening her world.

FOR THE LOVE OF A DOG

Now I have clouds too, albeit with different origins. My recent implosion sits on my shoulder, sometimes quiet, sometimes hissing, its breath hot in my ear. I carry a new frailty. I think I would understand my mother better now. I think I would be kinder. More patient. A better daughter. The daily business of living can be so tough, and I couldn't see it. Refused to see it.

As the countdown to dog ownership continues, trepidation builds alongside my excitement. I reach for my credit card. A sure sign of panic.

This is what I buy:

1. **A puppy training manual.**
2. *Three* **dog cages**, or 'crates' as they are called. The first came from a friend, but it was too big to fit under my kitchen table and I didn't have the heart to tell her, so I bought a medium-sized one online. But then, when I was trying to assemble the medium-sized one – for practice – I managed to render it unusable by using pliers to break all the

vital metal bindings holding the thing together, having mistaken them for part of the most formidably resilient packaging I have ever come across. It took hours, even with the pliers, and blistered my fingers – having been designed to be dog-destruction-proof, of course. Doh. Realizing my error, I am not sure I have ever felt more stupid. I had to curl into a ball on the kitchen floor until the worst of the mortification had passed. Then I hid the destroyed medium-sized crate in the cellar, next to the too-big crate, and ordered another medium crate from a different website, to avoid possible confusion or awkward questions.

3. *Two* 'puppy carriers'. The first is like a front-loading rucksack, for those early pre-vaccination weeks when the puppy and I fancy a bit of fresh air and her paws still aren't allowed possible contamination by the outside world. The second is a zip-up, oblong boxy one with a handle. Think Mary Poppins. This is for safe confinement of my puppy in the car when we visit the vet for injections and friends for cups of tea, handy for containing any unexpected explosions of body fluids.

4. *Three* dog beds. One for the kitchen, one for the hall and an eye-wateringly expensive deluxe tartan one for the TV room because that is where the puppy will want to spend most of its time, since she will be forbidden from going on the chairs or sofa.

(I am tempted to stop this list. It is making me feel faint. I could press delete. I may yet do so. No one would know. I am ashamed of my extravagance, my dumb, rigid plans. I can sense my mother's reaction, her eyes wide with disapprobation. Like all of her generation, she had an abhorrence of waste, whether it was money or chicken bones. Kit for her own dogs never extended beyond a collar, lead, bed and bowl. Toys were old tennis balls and sticks. But on we go.)

5. *Lots* of toys. Teething toys. Soft toys. Ball toys. Pulling toys.
6. A *mega* pack of puppy training pads. These are large, padded, highly absorbent squares. Think Pampers, but flattened. The

ingenious idea is you scatter them around whichever floor you are trying to protect and the puppy knows that this is the exact spot where it is supposed to relieve itself.

7. *Jumbo* **pack of antiseptic wipes.**

8. *Three* **leads.** Puppy size, dog size and a training lead, extra-long and guaranteed to tie itself, and all users, in knots.

9. *Two* **collars.** Puppy size and dog size, the latter a nice bright blue one, emblazoned with her name and my mobile number so that all nutters and dognappers will have no trouble taking note...

10. **A metal puppy pen.** Eight-sided, very heavy, in parts for assembly. This is so the puppy will be able to play safely in the garden while I attend to Other Important Matters.

11. **A stair gate.** Just one, though I fought the urge to buy several. For the stairs. For the kitchen. For the sitting room. There are so many places I do not want the puppy to go. Tiger Lily also will need Escape Passages and Areas of Safety.

12. **A faux-fur doggy rug.** So luscious, I could easily wear it as a shawl. It is for the sofa, just in case the puppy decides to jump on it from time to time, en route to her deluxe bed.

13. **Poo bags. Puppy food. Puppy dishes. Dog dishes.**

14. **Biological washing powder.** According to my puppy training book, which I study assiduously most days now, only biological powder will do for clearing up pee and poo. Any other detergent, and a trace of scent will remain, inviting the pup/dog back to the scene of the crime, to repeat the offence ad infinitum.

15. **Anti-chew spray.** XL size.

16. **A harness.** The puppy book mentions that these put less pressure on the neck than a collar when training.

17. **A quick-dry dog towel.**

18. *Two* **large, beautiful, expensive, woven, washable, water-repellent indoor doormats.** One for the front door, one for the back. Ha! I wasn't born yesterday. My pooch may be blessed with lovely short crimped hair and trim

little paws, but I have a new hall carpet to protect, not to mention freshly painted walls and skirting boards.

19. **A raffia toy chest.** For all the toys, obviously.

A burglar would have assumed the occupier of the house was either certifiable or planning to start a shop specializing in dog accessories. Even at the time I was too ashamed to confess the extent of my purchases to a soul. I knew it was a reflection of my flaky state, that the acquisition of each dog product was a futile attempt to pin this new project down. To pin *something* down. I was scared. Life had caught me out and tripped me up. Ultra-preparation was my only way of trying to ensure that it didn't happen again.

On the plus side, some of what I bought proved useful, and all of it helped me sleep at night. At least I was doing something. Arming myself for the battle ahead. A battle with a pint-size poppet called... MABEL.

The name had pinged into my head one day when – for once – I wasn't thinking about it. It wasn't on any of my shortlists but I knew at once that it was right. Names matter. It's one of the first things you sort as a novelist when embarking on a novel. With characters satisfactorily christened, a story is far more likely to flow. And so it was with my pup. Once named, Mabel stopped being an idea and began to come to life: a seven-week-old Golden Doodle who was going to come and live with me, not just for Christmas, but to her – or my – dying moment.

When the Big Day finally arrives, the son and I travel west in a state of such enjoyable high excitement that I decide the puppy project has already proved its worth. It helps that the son is also an Ace Navigator. We stop in a pub for lunch, drawing out the fun of the excursion. The puppy handover itself is quick and professional. With the paperwork done, I am despatched to wait in the car, and Mabel is carried out to me by one of the handlers, a small dangling bundle. She is placed onto my waiting lap, which I have taken the precaution of covering with an old loo mat (it seemed appropriate). I have brought a soft grey donkey toy for her, chosen with great thought from my stash. As we set off, the Welsh rain starts to come down in sheets, lashing and hammering at the car, deafening. It is like being in a car wash.

Mabel is the same size as the toy donkey. She curls into a fluffball, tucking her teeny nose into the dip between my knees. My designated chauffeur takes a string of pictures before we set off, lamenting the shortness of the straw he has drawn. I can feel Mabel trembling. She is clearly afraid, in shock. And little wonder. In the space of two minutes, she has been wrested from everything she has ever known – her mother, the rough-and-tumble love of her eight siblings, and all the scents and shapes of her Welsh home. She is also lying on a loo mat with her face pressed very close to a donkey.

Up to this point I have resisted the whole 'dog mother' thing. The fashion for cossetting pets like babies has always left me cold. Eeew. Every time the lovely girl with the singsong voice referred to us as Mum and Pup, I cringed. I am not Mabel's mother. She is a dog, albeit one of eye-popping cuteness. I am collecting her from a breeder's in order to start a new life mostly in my kitchen, mostly in a cage, if I follow the instructions in my puppy training manual.

Sitting in the back of the car that afternoon, however, with Mabel so small and fearful in my lap, feeling her warm little body and her heart beating through my jeans, there is no denying that something akin to a maternal urge surges through me. The desire to love and protect. She is an innocent. She has no choice but to trust me. I want, with all my being, to honour that trust, to make it justified.

My brain flips me back three decades. Stepping out of a maternity hospital into a hot, busy, dusty street in downtown Buenos Aires, clutching my two-day-old firstborn in my arms. After the calm, quiet, disinfected sanctity of the hospital, the reality check of the rough rude world is visceral. The heat, the dirt, the roaring cars, the danger. It is only then that I see the new, daunting, never-ending challenge of parenthood that stretches ahead; the relentless responsibility of protection; the love, as awful as it is wondrous.

Speeding along the M4, wipers on full blast, the younger son's broad shoulders hunched in concentration, I know better than to share this memory out loud. My driver might fear his mother had lost the plot. Again. These days there is less family worry about my emotional state, and I want to keep things that way. I am making decisions again, even if they prove to be Wrong Ones. I am taking charge of my life. Mabel is not a baby and I am not her parent. But after a while, if you are lucky enough to live long enough, everything starts to remind you of something.

It takes over four hours to get home, by which time it is dark and the rain biblical. To my elation, the loo mat on my lap remains completely dry. Not one dribble of pee, poo or puke. Mabel is clearly a star. And when I plonk her on the back lawn, holding an umbrella over us and saying, 'Empty!' (you may laugh – the son certainly did – but everyone knows you need a trigger word for toilet performance and someone suggested this one) Mabel immediately performs a neat little squatting pee. Oh, the happiness. The pride. My doodle is a doddle.

Inside the kitchen the youngest and I sprawl on the floor cooing over our new charge as she potters and clambers, lurching between timidity and boldness at every first encounter with her new environs. A spotty oven glove hanging from a hook stops her in her tracks. A feather is a playmate. We are for scaling and rolling on and burrowing under. The son and I are transfixed, smitten. We would gobble her up if we could. We take picture after picture, none of them quite seeming to capture the extent of her sweetness. Tiger Lily, predictably, is less impressed. She perches in prey-watch mode on the edge of the kitchen table, fur in spikes, eyes black. Whenever Mabel comes too close she shrinks and hisses, casting me looks of abject horror. I am just grateful that she is there, ballsy enough to engage with this new foe, albeit from the sidelines.

Mabel, happily, is oblivious to this animosity from her new life companion. The kitchen table is too high and there is too much else going on. Some specks of mud to eat. A blue teether toy to chew. (Yay, a toy she likes!) Cunningly, I have left the door of her cage/crate wide open, inviting exploration of its cosy interior – a big tatty cushion, a soft towel, yet more toys, strategically placed – but Mabel steers well clear of it. She prefers the old cat basket. She is also very keen on the discovery of her water bowl, mistaking it for a paddling pool.

'Retrievers are water dogs, after all,' says the son helpfully, as we watch Mabel plunging her paws in and out of the water, before attempting to get in the bowl itself, her evident delight increasing as she realizes this allows her to splash its contents up the walls and across the floor. The commotion is too much for Tiger Lily, who abandons her vulture pose and scrambles for cover in the TV room.

A few weeks after leaving the Argentine maternity hospital I make a long-distance call to my mother. The city is sweltering and there are power cuts, meaning no air conditioning. My baby and I are alone and have reached the end of our respective tethers. We are both slithery with distress, sweat and exhaustion. Both hollering.

'Pour yourself a large gin and tonic,' my mother instructs, her voice booming through the crackles and the horrible time lag of the many thousands of miles that separate us. The sound of her is so achingly familiar, so longed-for as I flounder in these early days of motherhood, that for a while I weep even harder. 'Check the baby is clean and fed and de-burped,' she commands, 'then take the gin to the other end of the house. Close all the doors. Put on the telly, or some music, very loudly. Drink the gin. Wait at least twenty minutes before you go back and check on him.'

I do exactly as I am told. Twenty minutes to the second. My son is sound asleep and stays that way for hours.

Mabel is a dog and my mother is dead. Nonetheless, it is this early baby advice that surfaces as I lie awake on Mabel's first night home, every sinew strained for the whimpering that is floating up from the kitchen. She is an eight-week-old ball of fluff the colour of clotted cream, and she is missing her real family and her first home. I didn't put her in her des-res cage in the end; I didn't have the heart. She clearly preferred the cat basket, so I left her in that, with the donkey and the favoured blue chew-toy and the loo mat, which I figured might have some traces of scents that were at least familiar. I tiptoed away, as one does with newborns. And as with newborns there was that gap of a few seconds, before the realization that she was alone dawned and the crying started.

I put my pillow over my head. I long to go down-stairs and cuddle my pup. Or better still, to bring her up to bed and make a cosy little nest for her in the doughy folds of my duvet. Loads of dog owners do just that. I know from all the anecdotes that have come my way in recent months. Just as babies aren't left to cry these days, neither are puppies. In one of the pet places Mabel and I go to now, the owner has a fancy little Pomeranian who sits on his lap all day and whom he has trained to kiss him on the lips. 'Kissy kissy!' he pleads, pouting, and the little doggie puts its paws on his shoulders and gives him lots of big licking smackers, right on the chops. I've also met a man in a park who boasted gleefully that his (huge) dog's face is the first thing he sees in the morning and the last thing he hugs at night because they sleep together under the covers.

Each to their own, but I don't want to share my bed with Mabel, or snog her for that matter. And if she is introduced to the option of being on a double bed on night one, she will want nothing less. And who could blame her? My bed is bloody lovely. *My* place of safety. A terrible pattern would be set. She would become exactly the spoiled, demanding, yelping creature I dread most. So I hunker down. I keep the pillow over my head. I picture toilet accidents spoiling the clean folds of my bed linen. And I cleave to thoughts of my mother, not just the leave-them-to-cry advice, but the generations of hounds she raised, happily incarcerated in her kitchen without a peep.

Within ten minutes Mabel has quietened. Loved ones die; we may or may not dream of them, but their voices live on, foghorns inside our heads.

★

I hurry down the following morning to find Mabel belly-flopped, half in and half out of the cat basket, all four paws at full stretch, chin flat on the floor. I assume she is dead. I am almost resigned – life is something that goes *wrong* – but in an instant she is in full-on awake mode, charging at me with all the doggy glee I had dreamed about. I am so delighted. She thinks I am GREAT. I go more bonkers than her. We roll around the floor together. I do not care that it is still only six in the morning, or that dotted *between* the puppy pads – placed with uncannily neat precision, one might say – are several piddle puddles and some tidy coils of excrement. When I eventually stop playing in order to clear them up – biological washing powder, mop in hand – Mabel joins in on her too-big springy paws, thinking it is a game. Things get messy. I give up and take her outside into the morning murk. I don't want to tell Mabel off yet. About anything. She is too diddy.

By mid-morning I feel as if I have been up for an eternity. I have cleared the kitchen and brought

Mabel inside. She isn't looking sleepy but I have things to do. Mabel may be the dearest small creature on the planet, but she must learn that there are other matters in the world besides her entertainment. I put the kettle on. Coffee. Maybe even a session at my desk. Life mustn't stop just because I have a puppy. As I reach for a mug Mabel totters to my ankles and promptly falls asleep, front paws and head stretched out across my feet. I have flip-flops on and her soft fur is warm on my skin. She is zonked. Dead to the world. I do not move. I stretch around the place to make my coffee. I drink it standing up. I try to drink quietly. I hardly dare breathe. All of the kitchen to choose from, including the beloved cat basket, and she chooses me. I am her Place of Safety. It makes me feel lucky. Chosen. Two things I had forgotten I could feel.

I would like to tell the man about my dog. I used to tell him everything. I miss that most of all, how we talked. I imagine phoning him sometimes. But what would there be to say, except 'Why didn't you love me enough?', and I don't think that is a question you can ask anyone. Love is not the product of a questionnaire. Feelings have all the power of facts. They cannot be 'right' or 'wrong'. They just are. If someone does not love you, no Q&A session in the world will sort it out. They do not love you. It is an absence of an emotion, not a crime.

The theory behind crate-training is that the puppy's mum will have taught it not to foul the area in which it sleeps. So if you lock the puppy in a cage over-night, it will know to control its bodily functions during that period. Six days in and the quantity and regularity of Mabel's overnight deposits (always between the pads) make this hard to believe, though she remains a sweet and eager squatter-on-command outside during the day. As the days tick by, I stagger downstairs earlier and earlier to try to forestall the problem. I slave with the mop and the biological washing powder. Both to no avail. The dawn starts grow less easy to enjoy. I curse Mabel as she frolics round the mop, skidding gleefully as I attempt to clean up her messes. Then, on day seven, my back 'goes' (I have a writer's back, stiff and twangy, very ill-disposed towards excessive use of hoovers, garden tools and mops). I can feel the dreaded despair lapping. Under a week and I am broken. I am as useless as I feared.

Desperation makes me willing to be cruel. The next night I make sure Mabel stays up late. I hobble round the garden at midnight, squeaking 'empty' till I'm hoarse. Mabel is more interested in disappearing into the shrubbery. Eventually I scoop her up (she fits in one hand) and plonk her on top of the tatty cushion that forms the centrepiece of her as yet unused cage. It is a large old stained velveteen thing of gaudy red and gold, brought back by one of the sons at the end of some term or other at uni. Mabel sits on it, a mini-princess on a gold throne, her big chocolate eyes blinking at me in puzzlement. What next in this new game? It's enchanting. Well worth a pic, but I am in a rush to get out while the going is good. I shut the cage door and bolt like a coward, fingers in my ears.

Halfway up the stairs I realize the kitchen is completely silent. It stays that way all night, and the next morning the gold cushion – the entire crate – is clean and dry. Released from her jail, Mabel shows no sign of trauma. She bounces at me with her usual delight and then skips after me into the garden, where she performs the longest toilet-squatting session of her short life. The next night I open the cage door and she trots in, curling up on the cushion of her own volition. Her second place of safety. We all need more than one.

Oh joy. Oh clever, good India, to teach her cub so well. And clever cub of mine, whichever one it was, to have inadvertently provided a smelly old cushion that puts my puppy so at her ease. Mabel loves my sons, their gentle throw-her-around games, their smell. Visits from them have been the highlight of her week. It's hardly rocket science that she would like cuddling up with one of their belongings.

I like it when things join up. When they make sense. It's all I'm searching for really. Writing novels, writing this, it's just an endless quest to connect all the dots, to produce a picture I can understand. When I understand things I am consoled. I feel strong.

4

Regrets

Mum's first dog was called Moojik. He was a squat white shaggy Lhasa Apso and she chose the name because it was a mountain in Tibet, she said, although nothing on Google will confirm this for me now. The Mooge, as we called him, was the most affectionate, eccentric and obstinate of dogs, beloved by my mother, who had waited out three decades of peripatetic diplomatic life before fulfilling the long-held desire to have her own hound. Moojik lived till I was in my mid-twenties and in latter years got so matted, so grumpy at the sight – let alone touch – of a grooming brush that Mum gave up entirely and resorted to the occasional severe snipping of the most knitted sections with scissors. Round his bum was the worst bit – hardest to get at as well as troublesome, thanks to the hazards of evacuating poo that has nothing but a tangle of fur through which to make its exit. To try to ward off such problems Mum developed and tutored a nifty technique of hoicking him up by the tail and doing a smart shake to encourage the poo to make it safely to the ground. If that failed, it was time to get the hose and rubber gloves out, an exercise which Moojik hated almost as much as the person having to do it. Oh lord, I loved that dog, but I grew to dread any dealings with his rear end.

A Lhasa Apso is not an obvious choice for a country dog. Even during his early, better-groomed days Moojik would spend much of the time looking like one of those sticky rollers designed to gather bits of debris and dirt. On walks he would also regularly decide that he had had enough and lie down on the path, beyond coaxing with either treats or love, until whoever was in charge caved in and carried him home. Though he was very much Mum's dog, Dad adored him too, primarily for his naughtiness. He would shout faux-fierce dog-orders at him in German, 'the language of cold command', as Dad liked to call it, chuckling in delight when Moojik took absolutely no notice. Best of all, late at night sometimes, when my father was in a waggish mood and Moojik was on their bed, angling to deter the inevitable command to retreat to his kitchen basket, Dad would talk softly and at length to him in English, about matters like the importance of sleep and being a good citizen, or any nonsense that came into his head. Moojik would sit rapt, while Mum, tucked up next to them, would shake her head in mock despair, loving every moment.

Happiness is wily. Things longed for are frequently disappointing, while the smallest, most unexpected events can provide joy. At our peril do we attempt to summon it to heel. Over the years I have learned to treat creative inspiration with the same respect. Nothing chases the muse so effectively beyond reach as the desire for its presence. It refuses to appear. It prefers to tiptoe up on you instead when your back is turned, startle you when you are wrung out from trying, the trying, as I have come to realize, being the key. Even in those rare, exquisite moments when inspiration does arrive, I know not to make any sudden moves, not to blow any trumpets. I treat it gently, skirt round it, let it breathe. Stare at the muse too hard, hold it too close, and it will be off again, a wet soap bar flying from my grasp.

A puppy is exactly the distraction I expected, the perfect reason not to worry about lack of inspiration or anything else. I am eager to train Mabel well, to love her, and for her to love me. But there is no instant 'happiness', no overnight cure for the meltdown desolation that resides still, deep in my gut, waiting to rise when it will, a tide with its own rhythms. Sometimes it just comes. At other times a piece of music will do it. Nothing catapults the heart like music. A song the man loved and my knees buckle. Or something – anything – by Louis Armstrong, who Mum was mad about, and my eyes brim. 'What a voice,' she'd swoon if ever the singer came up in conversation, her blue eyes darkening with an adoration that always held glimmers of mischief, '*what* a voice.' At Mum's wake we played Louis Armstrong on her CD player while we drank champagne, heady in that pocket of relief that follows an ordeal, even one that had rung out with celebration.

During the funeral one of my nieces sang the Bach/Gounod 'Ave Maria', a tune to make you weep at the best of times. It is a piece of deceptive simplicity that lifts you up, makes you soar and sets you down again. The sheer order of the Bach chords beneath the tune, the sense of control they provide, is comforting. Bach's notes know where they are going. We do not. As the niece performed, with a composure beyond her years, few in the church did not have their faces buried in hankies and tissues. I had just sat down from delivering the tribute and was in pieces anyway.

On a whim, I order the sheet music of this 'Ave Maria' off the Internet and begin, regularly, to play it on my piano. I play it for its beauty and how it reminds me of loving and losing Mum. I try singing too, but never make it past the first few words. You can't sing and cry; the throat is too closed up. With the songs the man and I shared I know better than to even try.

'How's it going?' the sisters ask, phoning regularly after Mabel's arrival, still casting their watchful eye. I know they confer behind my back too. Compare notes. I know I am supposed to be getting better. I have Mabel now. I *am* getting better. Time is doing its thing. But it can't be hurried.

I rave about Mabel. It is impossible not to rave about Mabel. A couple of weeks in and she still looks more like a cute toy than a dog, so pretty you don't want, ever, to stop looking at her. She has a little beard and gets excited by a buzzing bee or a leaf gusting across the grass. In the evenings I put her on my lap while I watch telly and she flops onto her back like a mini-sunbather, all four legs splayed, inviting me to stroke that hairless pot belly of a tum.

'I'm not enjoying the early mornings,' I confess to the sisters, aware that their hectic home lives and jobs mean they both leap out of bed at dawn. The brother, too, with his young family and city commute, is always on the move at first light. I am the spoiled stay-at-home, the novelist, the princess in her ivory tower. Physical exertion has for years meant a gentle jog, or a Pilates class, or chasing a train.

'And she's got bloody sharp teeth.' I look at my hands, dotted with little cuts and scabs, testimony to Mabel's at times painfully over-exuberant play. I have stopped consulting my dog book on this. I just yell – with genuine pain – and she desists, momentarily dismayed, until she forgets and does it again.

'But you don't regret getting her, do you?' the sisters urge.

'Oh, not for a moment. How could I regret her?'

No, I cannot allow myself to regret getting Mabel. But by week two, with the Welsh rain that followed us home still pelting, and not being able to take her anywhere, or get any work done, I am aware of a certain, contained level of panic. I must not fail at this new endeavour. My battered self-esteem couldn't cope. The abyss is there, still, in the shadows, jaws wide. It does not help that I am exhausted, unable to sleep thanks to the worsening state of my back. Every time the alarm goes off at its new ungodly hour, I long only to remain where I am. Through the gap in my bedroom curtains the sky is charcoal. I get up purely because I have to. Because Mabel needs me to. I picture her soft little tufty face at the bars of her cage, ears straining for the sound of my footstep. I imagine her anguish at needing to pee and poo. I reach for my clothes, moving gingerly to encourage my spine out of its lockdown.

Downstairs, I now need to perform a strange sumo squat in order to bend low enough to release the catch on Mabel's cage. She bounces out, a bundle of eager glee. I lever myself down till I am lying flat on the floor, so we can enjoy the reunion to the full. I stroke every inch of her. She is chubby and soft and full of wriggle. I tell her she is gorgeous. Her nuzzles with her small cold nose make me giggle. My dog book – my new bible – says it is important to get a puppy used to being touched, everywhere. But this is not why I can't keep my hands off Mabel. Handling her makes my heart buzz. It doesn't take a scientist to tell me those happy-chemicals are kicking in. I know that this is partly because she remains the sweetest puppy I have ever set eyes on, and partly because of the sheer tactile pleasure of physical contact with a fellow creature. When you are single and living alone, surviving on intermittent, treasured hugs from visiting loved ones, there is a basic, visceral pleasure in being jumped on daily, even by a small creature with razor teeth. I am also aware how important these physical games must be for Mabel, so recently torn from the merry dodgems-mayhem of her Welsh birthplace.

After the morning hello, I open the back door and Mabel shoots out into the garden, a woolly white bullet. She somersaults down the back steps, which she is supposed to be carried over (bad for a puppy's hips, my book warns) and bounds up the other steps (vet bills of squillions await me) onto the lawn where she performs her dear clever little toilet-squats. The book says to train a puppy to do its business in one discreet area of the garden, but I have long since given up on that. As far as I am concerned Mabel can relieve herself wherever the hell she likes so long as it isn't in the house. A first-time dog owner with a crocked back has to pick her battles.

And on it rains. Not since having bored toddlers to entertain have I examined the skies each morning so obsessively. Novelists love the weather. How the seasons manifest themselves is a vital ingredient for a good tale – a foil, a reflection, a context, or even a character in its own right. But faced with the reality of these two sludgy, drenching autumn weeks, I realize how thick the walls of my ivory tower have become. How used I have grown to staring at the weather through my big study windows. Watching the outside world from the inside. Describing it, rather than experiencing it.

Mabel loves being outside. She finds the rain interesting – cold wet stuff coming from the sky! She likes tearing at the grass with her scissor teeth and eating it. She also enjoys snacking on snails, pebbles, and rusty items (cans, nails) that she grubs for in the undergrowth. She requires constant vigilance and I am out of practice. Most of all Mabel loves mud. For digging. My increasingly rain-soaked lawn is becoming a heaven to her. She digs all over it, with the speed of a cartoon dog, earth flying, her paws and head disappearing as each hole deepens. After every session she looks like a coal miner emerging from an underground shift, eyes glistening in her blackened face, body dark up to her doggy elbows, comically stark against the rest of her honey-blonde coat. Each dig requires an after-session with the hose, performed on my knees because I can no longer bend over. Mabel likes the hose, which is a blessing, though mainly for eating. It goes without saying that I get wetter than my dog.

Soon my garden starts to look as if it is in the grip of some terrible disease. Every part of it is pock-marked with large holes or big brown scorched circles from Mabel's pee (it's the ammonia apparently). Between these lie countless little poo piles.

I scoop, but on she poops. Mabel is a poo machine. A bi-valve. Food goes in one end and comes out the other, with impressive efficiency. Each day I survey the scene of destruction and try to mind a bit more than I actually do. Part of me feels I *should* mind. But the truth is, it takes me back to being the mother of two young sporty boys ploughing up our various small gardens with whichever game was in favour or season. Hours and hours of exercise, fun and dirt. What are gardens for if not to be played in? Puppies, infants, it's all the same.

Tiger Lily is puzzled by the new outdoor activities. She creeps out of her private cat-flap and crouches in her new self-allocated place – the sidelines – hoping to remain unnoticed, her coat twitching in the drizzle. But Mabel always spots her. And when she does, her puppy-joy knows no limits. A playmate! At last! She lollops across the garden and dances in front of Tiger Lily, performing her best come-and-play moves, happily oblivious to the cat's expression of mounting horror. The moment – the inevitable moment – when Mabel gets too close, Tiger Lily delivers a swift, claws-out swipe to the side of the puppy's nose, spits cat-swearwords and skedaddles back through her flap. Each time it happens, Mabel is crestfallen. She sits back on her little bottom with a sigh, glancing at me for an explanation. Her biggest hope, to this day, is that Tiger Lily will morph into a pal. Mabel has no grounds for this hope. She is simply an optimist, in the purest sense, and it melts me every time.

I learn many things during these rain-lashed early days. I learn that a brolly isn't ideal when you are playing tag with a puppy, especially not if your back hurts and your umbrella is a small cheap flimsy handbag one that blows inside out at the first hint of wind. I learn that I do not own a proper anorak and that an emergency pocket-sized cagoule is no substitute. I learn that I no longer possess wellies and that some ancient padded après-ski boots retain no water-resistant qualities whatsoever. In short, I learn that while equipping the house with enough puppy equipment to start my own kennels, I have failed to equip myself. I also learn that nothing makes a poorly back worse than trying to peel off sodden socks while discouraging an equally sodden, mud-clogged puppy from traipsing the contents of its absorbent paws round the house. I start to keep an old towel by the back door, on the floor because there isn't a hook.

'Paw!' I say, hopefully, as Mabel and I wrestle with the towel, at least ten times every day, my thoughts flicking to all the dogs I have come across who have been taught how to 'shake hands' on just such a command. Mabel prefers to fight the towel. So I transfer the wrestling match to my lap instead, flipping her onto her back like a baby after a bath, noting, as her strength to resist me grows, that I am on borrowed time.

After Mum's last dog, Lucky, died, I remember telling her, firmly, ruthlessly, that she should waste no time in getting a replacement. Mum was seventy-nine. She had trouble doing things like getting out of her chair and bending down to open her fridge. In recent years she had also taken to falling over, as the elderly do, never quite recovering to the point of strength she had known before each tumble. One of the falls had happened when she was pulled over by a dog, the one before Lucky. She broke her shoulder on that occasion. Another time it was her wrist. On another, she fell backwards down some stone steps. The recoveries exacted a toll, not just physically, but mentally. We gave her a mobile phone to take when she was out, but she never got the hang of it. She would muddle it with the handsfree sets she had inside the house, making us laugh even as we despaired. Out walking with Lucky, she tripped over a few times but always made it home, with bruises like fireworks to show for her pains. Falling saps your confidence. You walk with fear, which – the irony of life can be so cruel – makes you even more likely to trip over your own feet.

I kept on at Mum about getting a dog. I did so because I hated opening the front door and hearing nothing but the hum of the telly. I was afraid of what old age was doing to her, where it would lead. If she stopped going on walks it was another milestone towards total defeat. I told her if she didn't feel up to getting a puppy, we could find another dog like Lucky, who had arrived aged seven, trained and docile, after her first elderly owner had died. When Mum still said no, I was cross. She was 'giving up', I ranted behind her back. A cat was found for her instead, a needy, quirky puss whom Mum at first complained was too much to manage. When I reminded her, with barely concealed incredulity, that cats were easy, that she had kept them for decades, usually more than one at a time, she looked sheepish. What I also thought, but did not say, was that it was good for her to have something to worry about other than herself. Which is true. Little did it cross my mind that within a couple of years, twenty-five years younger and pitched headlong by life's invisible tripwires, I would be telling myself the very same thing.

On the first sunny day I reach for the puppy carrier. The front-loading rucksack one. The other one (forget Mary Poppins; think small coffin with handle) has been used twice, once for a visit to the vet, and once for a trip to Pets At Home, both stressful because Mabel only desisted from crying if I kept a hand *inside* the carrier so she could rest her face against it. This made driving hard, and almost certainly illegal. As for Pets At Home, let's just say that all serving assistants and other customers must have breathed a sigh of relief when we left. Mabel may be small, but, as I am discovering, she has a shrill bark.

I had never expected Mabel to be that keen on the coffin – it was purely for the car – but I have high hopes for the front-loading doggy rucksack. 'Pop your puppy into your carrier and take it to as many different places as possible,' my new bible instructs. 'Shops! Bus stops! Hang around entrances to schools and stations!' (Without Mabel, the chance of being arrested would be high.) 'Use that puppy carrier every chance you get!' it goes on. 'Get your puppy socialized!'

This is what I want above all else. A well-adjusted, sociable dog, whom I can trust not to harry cyclists or joggers; a dog who won't, ever, sink her teeth into the forearms of two-year-olds. After two weeks I am also desperate, for my own sake, to get out of the house. My rigid spine responds well to exercise (hence the history of jogging and Pilates) – it loosens the clench. In addition to which, Mabel, like babies, is most adorable when she is asleep, but never seems to sleep for long enough. Awake, she is a full-time job, distressed if left alone too long, or determined to poison herself on detritus from the garden. She wants, always, to be played with. Her favourite game is tug-of-war. My book says this is because it helps soothe her sore gums and teething puppy teeth. But there are only so many tug-of-war games a woman can take, let alone one with a dodgy back.

At first Mabel thinks the puppy carrier looks like fun. It has snazzy colours and lots of zips and straps. Too many zips and straps. They are confusing. Mabel's paws are mini-spades, and her legs, I suddenly notice, are getting remarkably gangly, not ideal for folding into a bag, which, as I gradually realize, is essentially what is required. It also becomes apparent, after some tussling, that the peephole supposedly designed to accommodate Mabel's head is way too small. Even a chihuahua would struggle. I have bought the wrong size carrier. By now clocking what I am trying to do – stuff her into a bag – Mabel starts to resist in earnest. But I am not prepared to admit defeat. The sun is shining and I want to take my puppy for a walk to enjoy it. I am also experiencing a mounting need to prove I am Top Dog. Many sources have iterated the importance of this. Surrender on one matter, and who knows what chaos will unfold.

If I can just get *enough* of Mabel in the bag, I decide, we will be fine. Then we can get going and she'll calm down, get the hang of things. I cling to the clear, enticing picture of how good this walk could yet be: Mabel's dear little hairy face with its floppy cinnamon-tipped ears and jet bobble-nose poking out of the carrier; people of all ages stopping to swoon and stroke; Mabel enjoying the sights and sounds as we bob along, nodding off perhaps, as the boys used to do when they were wee and being similarly carted about.

By ignoring the head-hole, I eventually get most

of Mabel zipped into the bag. I grip her with both arms to keep her in position. I talk to her. I tell her what a great time we are going to have. I get us into the street, but Mabel doesn't settle. A bus lumbers past, and in her terror she almost ejects herself vertically from my clutch. I see squashed puppy. It would only take seconds. I try to zip more of her into the bag, but she has become a squirming octopus. She doesn't like the other traffic either, or a cawing crow, or aeroplanes, or the clank of scaffolding poles. Not liking things intensifies Mabel's efforts to escape. I pop treats in her mouth. I clasp her more tightly. I am getting very hot and tense. I am starting to hate the sun. A man approaches who wants to say hello. Mabel wants to say hello too, by scrambling onto his chest. He tries to stroke her, asking all the questions I have subsequently grown so used to – what breed, what age, what sex – but it is hard for both of us because Mabel's shark teeth keep catching on his fingers.

'Sorry – puppy teeth!' I cry, hurrying us away. When I see a mother and some children approaching, interest already stoked at the cute squirming contents of my bag, I scuttle across the street. They will try to stroke Mabel and she will chew their hands. She might draw blood. I will be sued and Mabel will have to be put down. I take us home at a run, which Mabel, understandably, hates even more than the walking. I am drenched in sweat. Defeated.

Mabel is ecstatic to be back in the kitchen. Out of the bag. She leaps and rolls and tumbles, expressing her delight, breaking off only to do a long pee in the middle of the kitchen floor. I mop it slowly. I do not tell her off. She is only ten weeks old and she didn't like being zipped into a bag. I don't blame her. I trudge down to the basement with the carrier, placing it on top of the pile of other abandoned equipment.

The next day the sun shines again. New dawn brings new energy, new hope. I have another card up my sleeve. The puppy 'playpen'. I picture Mabel larking around safely on the lawn, while I do things like call my agent to find out how the submissions for my new novel are going. I tell myself my old life is waiting in the wings, requiring only to be grabbed hold of. The pen is fun to build, in spite of its eight heavy panels and Mabel's determination to eat the instructions. For all my lack of robust physicality, I have always enjoyed a good construction project: flatpacks from Ikea, Lego kits, even a Playmobil set and I have to make a conscious effort not to elbow a toddler out of the way to assemble it first. I suppose it's the buzz of satisfaction at slotting things into their rightful place. The same reason I like crosswords. And writing novels.

The playpen offers considerably more space than the hateful puppy carrier, but Mabel's enthusiasm for the project still evaporates the moment I place her inside it. She starts to bark and won't stop, not even when I lob in toys and balls. Not even when I busy myself deadheading roses that don't need deadheading. Not even when I go indoors to put the kettle on, thinking yet again about motherly advice and screaming babies and how if left for long enough any living creature will give up and go quiet. Not even when I tell myself I am Top Dog.

Instead, I begin to think how much the noise will be pissing off my neighbours. It also occurs to me that I am steadily cultivating exactly the needy yapper of a dog I had been warned of and so dreaded.

While Mabel gambols and rejoices round my ankles I dismantle the pen and lug all eight panels, one by one (they are heavy), down to the basement. The pile of rejected puppy gear has become a pagoda. By the time I am done, my locked spine has reached shouting point. Mabel flops at my feet, exhausted by the morning's fun, and I reach for my phone. I should call my agent but I don't feel up to it. When it comes to book submissions, no news is always bad news. Instead, I make an appointment with a physiotherapist and then embark on a serious google of puppy training classes in my area. Yet again, I am not managing. I need help. From professionals.

The last time Mum came to visit I took her to the theatre, a treat we had enjoyed scores of times over the years. We went to a play she had specifically asked to see, with Bill Nighy in the lead role. Mum had a real soft spot for Bill Nighy. Indeed, any mention of the actor prompted expressions of mischievous delight similar to those evoked by Louis Armstrong. Gregory Peck had the same effect.

The play baffled her. It was a kitchen drama, and she was beyond comprehending what all the quick-fire conversation was about. What struck me most powerfully, however, was a moment in the interval when we were making our way to the bar. She didn't want a drink – she had her bottle of water – but was accompanying me because I did want one. Badly. She tottered next to me among the elbowing crowds, clutching her handbag and her bottle. And then suddenly, somehow, an elbow or a jostle proved too strong and she lost her balance. I caught her as she fell, in time to right her again. I looped my arm firmly through hers for the rest of the way, carrying her bag and her water for her, keeping pace with the crowd instead of trying to beat it. What haunts me now isn't just my selfishness – it was a hot, packed theatre and she was eighty-one and didn't want to go to the bar! No, what really haunts me is how light she felt as I stopped her falling. Light as air. As if her bones were already empty. Hollow. Five months later she died.

I am not big on regrets. I don't really believe in them. Life demands decision-making, and sometimes, with hindsight, we can see that the roads we have chosen were unwise. One can only work with the knowledge, wisdom and emotional state one has at the time. So I have always tried to learn from bad decisions, but seldom wasted energy regretting them. When I think of Mum, however, something like regret clouds my heart. Two weeks into Mabel-ownership and I am on my knees. Mum was struggling to open her small fridge and had the bone density of a feather. Yet I had seriously believed her capable of managing a new dog and fighting her way through hordes at a theatre bar. The regret-cloud is because I cannot undo how I was. Because it has taken the loss of her for me to start to see her, and myself, clearly.

5

Discipline & Surrender

When Mabel passes the milestone of her final vaccinations my elation knows no bounds. She is a free pooch! We can go on walks like normal dogs and owners! The course of puppy training classes is booked but does not start for several weeks. In the meantime I place all my faith in my now dog-eared (some adjectives are too irresistibly apt) bible. In truth, I become obsessed with how to train a dog. How to mould Mabel. I talk and think and dream of little else.

I know it is too much. I know I am still not of sound mind. The siblings, the sons, the close friends, humour me. Dog talk is safe ground for all of us. They want to keep my gaze averted from the past, as do I. Increasingly, there are things to avoid in the present too. Like the rejections of my novel, trickling steadily in, hard fodder for light chat. Far worse is the continuing stalemate over Mum's estate. The lawyers' bills are rising. Our age-old clan closeness is being tested to the limit. Without resolution, we are a family in limbo. Eighteen months on, Mum's house, full still of her belongings, her life – our childhoods – hangs like a moment frozen in time. The same ornaments, books, pictures, the countless family photographs, sit exactly as she left them on the morning she walked out of the house expecting to return. The same cobwebs dangle in the eaves. The same dusty bottles lie in the cellar. The house, all of us, are in a state of suspension. Half dead, half alive. It is no way to be.

Alone too, I still have to work hard at looking ahead. Every temptation to glance backwards hurts. To Mum. To the man. He may have walked away, but oh, how I miss him. I feel it all over, a dull ache beneath my skin. Falling in love with another human being is not something we choose. It happens *to* you. And when it does, it puts the world into Technicolor. Green is greener. Blue bluer. It energizes. It inspires. We are our best selves. It is also a surrender. An abdication of control. You are at the mercy of your love. You open the doors of your heart, doors you may well have vowed to keep closed. You say to your new beloved, look, here is the soft inner beating space of me. My core. I am entrusting its safety to you.

The truth is, I am a damaged dog owner. My core has been pulped. I trusted when I should not have done so. When it was not safe to do so. Because love is never safe. Which I suppose is the essence of its power.

Love isn't safe, and I am aware that my all-consuming need to control Mabel is not wholly about controlling Mabel. It is about me. There is a logic to it: namely, that if I stay in command of the nitty-gritty of my life, of my dog, neither can let me down. I cannot be hurt. I cannot again be ridden roughshod over and left, bleeding, by the side of the road. I understand this sort of stuff. For thirty years it has been my literary terrain. How humans suffer; how they do harm to one another; their endless misunderstandings, miscommunications and betrayals; the sunbursts of sublime connection that make it all worthwhile. How, if we fail in one area, we pressure ourselves harder in another. The emotional webs we spin. Oh yes, I am good on all of that. I get it. What we all want and need. Why it is so very hard for us to find. The struggle to love and be loved. The fragility of trust. I have processed it on the page. I am processing it now. Yet no amount of processing provides armour against pain. Sometimes I think it even makes it worse. I dwell on things in order to disentangle them. I can't stop looking at them, can't stop trying to find answers.

The other, more prosaic reason behind my drive to control Mabel is because, as I quickly realize, she is very likely to suffer – or cause – death or injury if I don't. This is not just because she is a lunatic puppy with a taste for rusty nails and dead snails that may have eaten lethal slug pellets. It is because I live in a city. The enormity of the challenge this presents is only just sinking in.

In Rome I had naively worried that a town dog didn't have enough space, but as I embark on my first, longed-for 'proper' dog walks, with Mabel tripping over her paws, chewing ardently on her crisp new leather lead, I see suddenly that there is too *much* space in a city, all of it crammed with things that have the power to maim or destroy an out-of-control puppy. My book says to allow your dog time off the lead from the get-go, to encourage her to learn about following you and coming when you call. But this takes courage when the puppy in question is in a constant state of investigative overexcitement and barely knows her own name, and when it dawns on her owner that, though biggish, their local park – like all London parks – is humming with activity and also – like many London parks – open on all sides to busy roads. If Mabel takes off, I am powerless to stop her. She is an accident trying to happen.

And boy, does Mabel want to take off. All the time. Everywhere. Towards everything and every-body. Traffic is the least of my worries. Before reaching the busy roads there are myriad other hazards in Mabel's path, or rather, Mabel is a hazard in theirs. Toddlers. Cyclists. Joggers. Walkers. Shoppers. Picnickers. Canoodlers. Footballers. Frisbee-ers. Rugby players. Keep fit groups. Taekwondo classes. Personal trainer sessions. Fragile old people. People terrified of dogs (I wish they could wear signs). Quite apart from the temptations of dropped litter, scurrying squirrels, foxes and fox poo (for rolling in). But worst of all distractions, as a hazard and as a temptation, are OTHER DOGS.

London is Dog City. I cannot believe I have hitherto failed to notice this. Our capital is a canine quagmire. It teems with the beasts: big, little, vast, medium, shorn, hairy, scary, wiry, snarly, bouncy, wild, wary, waddling, grizzled, grumpy, off-lead headcases, on-lead snappers, as well as all the bounding beautiful mutts who want to lead Mabel astray as much as she wishes to be led. The nub of the problem is that Mabel, aged twelve weeks, has no powers of discernment. Indeed, she wants to engage with every single creature that crosses her puppy radar, regardless of their size, ferocity level or reciprocal enthusiasm for engaging with her.

The sight of another dog is like a drug to Mabel. She belts off. She goes loopy. She cannot help herself. She has laser vision. If I do not stay one step ahead and clamp the lead on every time another animal appears on the horizon, I am in constant pursuit, yelling and being ignored as Mabel bombs across the park. Every walk becomes a run. I find myself thinking, often, of the man who chased Fenton in Richmond Park, to the amusement of millions, myself included, when the clip went viral. I have become that man. Every day.

There is no respite. If Mabel isn't actually chasing other dogs she is laying herself in their paths, flat on her back, legs spreadeagled, inviting close inspection of the dear little rusty patch of fur protecting her private parts. I am not dumb. I know that this is 'submission', a wise tactic, at least in doggy parlance. It nonetheless throws a certain ironic light on my pre-puppy worries over gang rape. Mabel looks as if she is hot for any action she can get. Some of the dogs clearly think so too. It can make for interesting conversations with their owners. Mabel at three months is begging for sex.

If I am not careful I will have puppies on my hands. I couldn't cope with puppies. I am barely coping with Mabel. I consult my bible. It says it is advisable to allow a female dog at least a couple of 'seasons' (periods) before neutering, so that she can get in touch with her inner feminine doodah. I consult my vet, who says there's evidence both ways and it's up to me. I like my vet. I tell her I want to have Mabel's uterus removed at the earliest legal opportunity. She says that's at seven months and books me a slot. Sorry, but sometimes a damaged dog owner has to recognize her own limitations and put them first.

Many years ago, when the youngest was in the final throes of his Get A Dog campaign, he wrote a list of 'For' and 'Against' points and left it on my desk. The 'Against' column contained merely two apposite remarks – *Cat unhappy* and *Harder to go on holiday* – while the 'For' column was chock-a-block. The son is a smart and conniving cookie and took some resisting. Suddenly coming across this list again during a rare spell at my desk – there has been no sign of the muse for a long while now – makes me sit up.

Healthy
New idea for book/blogs
Puppy tweets
Facebook pictures
You may actually love it
May make dog friends…

He was still a teenager. He knew nothing of the thickening of the walls of my ivory fortress. Nor did I. Just as he had no crystal ball to show when his grandmother would die or how his mother would implode under the pressure of the coincidence of that loss and a romance gone wrong. He didn't know my sixteenth novel would hit a wall. At the time his suggestions about tweeting and blogging had made me laugh out loud. I didn't have a Facebook page then, let alone a Twitter account. Nor did I nurture any secret intention or desire to write about a dog. I was a novelist, a crafter of fiction, inspired by humans not animals. I was riding one of the best crests of my life. Independent. Happy. Loneliness was still just a word. I did not need a bridge back into the world, or to anything else.

Studying the son's list in my new circumstances, I am struck not just by the uncanny prescience of my second-born, but by the inherent truth of his observations. A dog of any age needs to be taken out, ergo you will become healthier. Just as a puppy will be fallen in love with and cry out to be photographed, written about, tweeted about and therefore find itself, from time to time, taking star position in postings (or books).

And as for *May make dog friends*, it is simply impossible – IMPOSSIBLE – to move around the outside world with a three-month-old Golden Doodle puppy in tow and not make new acquaintances. Particularly if that puppy is Mabel, whose love of her own kind is matched only by her passion for humans. For Mabel's sole aim in life – from day one – has been to introduce herself not just to every dog she sees, but to every single person too. Every. Single. Person. When not dog-chasing across the park, therefore, I find myself talking to other people. Strangers. The shortest of circuits takes us hours. Humans are so friendly! Many change their own routes just to say hello. Every one of Mabel's and my excursions is action-packed. Like loony cocktail parties. Suddenly I am having more conversations in a week than I have had in a year. It is not always easy. Sometimes I want to run away. I am an oyster being prised open. Mabel is the pearl. Sometimes it hurts. But I know it is 'good for me'. And because it is all about Mabel, I have no choice.

Every time I drop a glance at my new life companion I understand why all this new social interaction is taking place. Being with Mabel is like hanging out with a film star. A miniature film star rocking a wavy honey-cream coat, a tufty beard with wheat-coloured highlights, and a puppy lollop that contains the dearest hint of a John Wayne swagger. When talked to, she cocks her head, her caramel eyes intense, soulful, as if she has seen something of the world now and knows it contains surprises, not all of them welcome. Her eyelashes are the longest I have ever seen on a dog, gingery coloured and arranged in the perfect curved gradation of a feather. Her nose has somehow got blacker, shinier and broader, losing its early poodle-pointiness. The nostrils set into it are deep and clear, twitching every time she spots something, getting the measure of it through her astonishing powers of smell. It is the nose of a hound.

The rest of her is all about the hair, a mop of white dreadlocks exploding out of her poodle dome-topped head. Her ears, floppy and crinkled, dangle out of this chaos, bouncing round the curves of her face like a bob-cut hairdo. Their once neat apricot tips have spread into shaggy tasselled fringes of light rusty brown, a blend of shades of which any hairdresser would be proud. Balancing this drama with absurd and perfect symmetry is Mabel's tail. It is a retriever tail gone mad, a fountain of smooth long hair, forever pointing skyward, as resplendent as a plume on a royal Life Guard's helmet.

No wonder people ogle. I am the hanger-on who got lucky, the person sharing a popularity she does not deserve. I knew when I chose Mabel that she would be a pretty dog. I just had no idea how pretty, nor the extent of the attention this would draw.

As a novelist you grow used to invisibility. You slave at it. A good story should stand independent of its creator. If characters appear like puppets on strings, you have failed. In life, however, it is our visibility that keeps us connected and sane. As the years pass we move from one public role to the next – as children, partners, parents, lovers – and each role throws out paths for us to follow or reject, scripts to read from or rewrite. If too many of those roles are taken away or become obsolete – no matter how we may have chafed at them – we can start to feel invisible. That we don't matter. It is hard not to flounder. With no outer roles to follow or rail against, we are left with only ourselves. On good days it feels like freedom. On bad days it is a prison. It dawns on me that this is why old age can be so hard, so isolating. Isolation breeds isolation. You get visited, but that is not the same. Visitors, even if they are family, always leave. I find myself wondering what the time between all our visits was like for Mum, how bad it got. I hate to think she ever felt invisible, or that she did not matter. She always mattered. She matters still.

Every so often, one of Mabel's and my daily encounters turns nasty. There are scary dogs out there – neglected, locked up, abused, trained to attack – and even scarier owners. Mabel is gormless still, an innocent. She ploughs into trouble and I follow, becoming a version of myself with which I have not hitherto been acquainted, brave and foolhardy. I yell. I wade in. I grab slathering beasts I do not know by the collar in order to rescue Mabel from the mêlée. The owners are invariably dismissive. Defensive. They use cosy words like 'grumpy' or 'bossy' to describe the behaviour of their charges, or claim, scornfully, that they were only wanting to 'play'. Yeah, right. Well, Mabel and I may still be getting to know each other, but I can state with absolute conviction that my puppy's idea of a leisure activity does not involve being pinned to the ground by a snarling adversary while she yowls in terror.

I grow better at spotting likely trouble: dogs running wild, or on short double leads (harness and neck), owners absorbed with their mobile phones. It is like scanning a playground as a parent. You check for potential bullies. You want your offspring to feel free, but you always have their back.

Mum never took her dogs to a park. Their daily walks were on the common opposite her house. For a treat, maybe twice a year, they would be put in the car and taken to some woods a couple of miles away. She didn't worry about socializing them, or training them to do anything except come home, often in their own good time. She would leave the back gate open by way of encouragement. Her biggest worry was adders. On hot days she would do her walks in the cool of early morning and late on in the evening so as to minimize the chance of disturbing one, coiled unseen in the bracken. It was the heat that made them dangerous, she said. They slept too deeply to have time to get out of your way. She had a cache of horror stories about what bites from these snakes could do – to dogs and people – but in the end never had to face the problem herself. Testimony, perhaps, that her theories and precautions worked.

Mum preferred walking at antisocial times anyway. The notion of a dog being a handy vehicle for meeting other people would have been anathema to her. She would have pooh-poohed the very idea, reiterating in tones of bafflement that her ideal walk was one when she didn't meet a soul. Dad had felt the same. They both said it was being diplomats that had done it. After four decades of making small talk and shaking hands with semi-strangers, all they wanted was to be left alone. With each other. Which was why it didn't work so well after Dad had gone. That was when Mum began to falter, even though she had twenty years left to go.

One day a man comes to chop down a tree in my garden. Mabel is beside herself with the excitement of it. She likes men best and always misbehaves most horribly with them. I blame the sons and their giddy rough-and-tumble games which she so adores. Mabel leaps at the tree man in a frenzy and will not leave him alone. When I shout at her she rushes to the one flowerbed she knows she is not allowed on and starts digging tunnels. When I yell harder she gets even more excited and digs more furiously. Whereupon I lose the last shreds of my cool and try to catch her – listen up, people: never chase a puppy; they think it is FUN – and she charges off, a maniac now, tearing up more plants as she goes, barking, mud-soaked, ecstatic at her own naughtiness. Never has she behaved quite so appallingly. But worst of all for me is my awareness of the tree man watching, the burn of humiliation.

There have been other such moments of public shame over the weeks: an incident in a garden-designer friend's treasured lily pond, another in a park pothole the size of a paddling pool when I had a ringside audience of other dog owners, all in stitches, Mabel emerging on both occasions like some creature from the deep, dripping slime. But this business in the garden takes me to a new low. Weeks of home training and all I can do is make Mabel 'sit' for a treat and 'wait' before wolfing her dinner. I am a powerless, useless dog owner, doomed to be pitied and laughed at for the next decade. Maybe less if the puppy hip joints I've allowed my garden steps to ruin don't bring her down first.

After the tree has been chopped and I am writing a cheque and Mabel is slumped, exhausted from her antics, the dirt that was once on her body spread around the kitchen floor, the man starts talking to me about dogs. It turns out he has several, which is cheering to hear, since it at least partially explains Mabel's mania. The scents on him will have driven her nuts. I confess to the man that I am having disciplining problems – as if he needed telling – whereupon he proceeds to disclose, in the manner of one passing on a secret from the Magic Circle, a trick that involves rattling a plastic bottle or tin can full of stones when a dog misbehaves. The rattling noise is terrible to them, he explains solemnly. They stop whatever they are doing at once. Indeed, he warns, if used wrongly or too much it can seriously stress a dog out. With his own pack, he says, he has only to glance at his plastic bottle of stones and they behave like lambs.

I am impressed. I am thrilled. To make Mabel behave by looking at a bottle! Or a tin! I am a great fan of trusting people who know whereof they speak. We cannot all be good at everything. I can string sentences together; other people understand cars. Or boilers. Or drains. Or dogs. That is why Mabel and I have puppy training booked and why it can't start soon enough.

Only idiots let dumb pride get in the way of consulting experts. Twenty-eight years earlier I had begged the one midwife who seemed capable of calming my wailing newborn to come to my house for a coaching session in her skills. I can see her now, cool in the humid sweat of the South American summer, draping my tiny furious baby belly-down over her forearm and gently tapping his back with her fingers, while his small curly legs and arms relaxed and swung freely. I watched avidly, certain that if only I concentrated hard enough, replicated exactly enough – if only I could do it *right* – then my perplexed, squirming infant would never know another moment's distress. I was wrong of course. The poor mite got colic and didn't like the swelter, made worse by the power cuts that prevented us from using air conditioning. But I never forgot the way that dear nurse held him, and I used it hundreds of times to good effect in the years that followed.

As soon as the tree man has gone, I empty out six mini tonic cans (resisting the urge to pour them into a tumbler with a slosh of gin), gather a mound of small stones from the garden and carefully feed them into the cans, sealing the tops with tape. Mabel potters round with me, intrigued. She is all meekness now, a castigated toddler. I go to the top of the house to experiment. Mabel is not allowed upstairs and I want her out of earshot in case she gets upset. The rattling is pleasingly horrendous. For a moment I feel afraid for Mabel. She is clearly somewhat highly strung. Maybe I am about to turn her into a neurotic mess. Or maybe I am about to create the most obedient dog in London. I return to the ground floor and plant the little tins in strategic places, ready for grabbing. I can't wait to use them. I put one in my anorak pocket for walks.

When the youngest comes round for supper I get my chance. Mabel immediately leaps on him, and I hop around rattling a can in her face and shouting 'Off!' and 'Down!' and probably some other, unrepeatable things too. The son is appalled. The noise is truly blood-curdling. Each rattle stops Mabel in her tracks for a good nanosecond, then she jumps again, prompting me into action too. The son begs me to stop. He says he likes being jumped on and I appear to have lost my mind.

Over the next couple of weeks I try with other visitors – warning them in advance where I can – but the only person getting stressed out by the process is me. Mabel clearly starts to think that cacophony is an integral part of celebration. If anything it makes her wilder.

Out walking proves just as hopeless, albeit for different reasons. I discover that striding along with a can of stones in your pocket means you… rattle. All the time. Mabel casts me sidelong looks of bemusement. I try padding gloves and tissues into my pocket to muffle the noise, but it makes no difference. I am a walking maraca. I have a couple of goes at shaking the can when she jumps on strangers, but quickly realize it triggers more alarm than the jumping. Victims eye me as if considering making reports to social services, or the RSPCA, an easy enough option given how my mobile number blazes from Mabel's collar.

I surrender. I throw the cans away. 'Foiled again, Emily,' as my mother would say. Though why, or who Emily was, I haven't the foggiest and never did. I wish I had asked her. Why didn't I ask her? Children accept so much, and only think to try to make sense of it years afterwards. The longer Mum is gone, the more she is filling my head, not as the person we looked after, but as the one who looked after us. I hear her voice with greater and greater clarity, its exact inflections, all her funny sayings; snippets of her, floating up from the past. 'Arrffle, arrffle, arrffle,' she would chuckle at babbling babies, or anyone she thought was talking enjoyable nonsense. Or 'Piddly in the garden!' a shrill singsong instruction only ever deployed for Moojik, as the pair of them danced round the apple tree under the Sussex moonlight. 'Sick transit Gloria Tuesday' (spelled as I heard it) was another, thrown out for reasons which, again, I never understood or thought to question. Only now – now! – do I realize that of course it was a jokey reference to 'Sic transit gloria mundi'. *Thus passes the glory of the world*. Yes, Mum, so it blooming well does.

If I had had the chance to tell her about this book she would have dismissed the notion of being worth a mention, while secretly being rather pleased. She would also have marvelled that the acquisition of a puppy could prompt the outpouring of so many words. She would have rolled her eyes. She would have laughed. It would have made her happy.

6

The Dating Game

There are things that remind me of the man. Scattered here and there. Small, silly things. Hair triggers for memories. I should gather them up. Put them away. Burn them, maybe. It is hard to be the one who is left. By the dying, by the deserting. It is all the same. We know we should let go. But we cling on.

One day I catch a glimpse of myself side-on – a chance reflection in a mirror-in-a-mirror – and it makes me afraid. I see someone I do not recognize. Someone with unkempt, half-frizzed hair, in dirty flat shoes, ancient unflattering jeans and a shapeless old jumper. There is no speck of make-up on her face, not even a sweep of eyeliner along the upper lids, a minimal act of enhancement ruthlessly adhered to for years by way of demonstration – to myself at least – that I had not given up completely, that I was still in the game.

But now, if there ever was a game – and I'm not sure there was – I am clearly no longer in it. My body, rickety back notwithstanding, is okay – I even have a few new muscles thanks to Mabel – but in terms of appearance, I have somehow toppled off the proverbial cliff. There has been no conscious decision to 'let myself go'. Indeed, throughout my life I have tried hard not to. Looking after oneself outwardly helps inwardly, I have always found. Self-respect. Pride. We do not need an audience for such things to matter. But the new reality of Mabel has been chiselling away at my efforts. Why wear nice clothes when they are to be ruined by muddy paws? Why wash and dry irritatingly fine hair when it is going to be rained on or wind-blasted out of shape? Why trace a line of black kohl along eyes that are going to start streaming the moment they come into contact with the chill of early morning air? The kohl makes them sting and go bloodshot.

The line becomes an inky dribble suggestive of someone who has been up all night in a bar brawl.

It is tempting not to care. I can aspire to bag-lady chic if I want to. Mabel is the perfect excuse. I have no one to impress, after all, no one who will observe me and give two hoots what they see. My daily perfume is eau de dog. And Mum always said that not giving a damn what the world thought was one of the luxuries of old age. When it came to clothes her preferred choice of gear – all year round – grew to be loose stretchy trousers and a baggy T-shirt. To her dying day she could brush up stunningly, turning heads, when required. But she never wanted to. Another legacy of the diplomatic circuit, she claimed, all those years of having to put on a show when one wasn't in the mood.

I am not in the mood either and cannot imagine ever being so again. But the outside world is beginning to knock, quietly, at my door. Rehearsals with my choir are starting. The *Messiah*. I love the *Messiah*. I also love going to the pub with my fellow singers afterwards. But Mabel is still too little to be left for long. She needs to be emptied. Played with. In short, I need a puppy-sitter. The youngest son volunteers a friend who is between jobs. I make sure there is beer and food in the fridge and leave out a twenty-pound note. I wash and style my hair. I put on nice clothes. Much to the consternation of Mabel, I warble 'His Yoke Is Easy' during the course of these preparations. It is a high fast chorus and I am a soprano; Mabel jerks out of a snooze the moment I start, clearly trying to work out whether I am in physical pain or speaking some new language she has yet to comprehend. I like singing, I tell her sternly, so you better get used to it. She lowers her chin back onto her paws, continuing to keep a weather eye, but not actually running away – or howling – which I decide to take as a compliment.

It is wonderful to be out of the house and dogless, wonderful to lose myself in the concentration required to tackle one of the greatest choral works ever written and then drink Guinness (ideal for soothing a tired throat) afterwards. During the course of the drinks I regale my tolerant singing companions with tales from the doggy front line and then find, suddenly, that I am eager to get home. A glorious welcome awaits me, from a floppy, happy puppy, the sitter having left, as instructed, after a couple of hours.

'She bit him,' the youngest phones to inform me the next day.

'That's impossible.'

'No, Mum, she really did. Badly. On the ankle. Drew blood. He was trying to put together some dinner and she wanted him to play.'

'Oh my God, poor boy. Is he okay?'

'Yep. Fine. But it bloody hurt, he said. I think he got pretty mad at her.'

'I don't blame him.'

'No. But probably best not to ask him again. I don't think he'd say yes. I mean, she *bit* him, Mum.'

'Yes. Of course. Tell him I'm sorry. I'll tell him too, of course.'

'I guess she only wanted to play.'

'Yes, but still. Hopefully puppy training will help.'

'Hopefully.'

The friend got a job soon afterwards so puppy-sitting ceased to be a career option anyway. The funny thing was Mabel's razor teeth were never so razor again. Whatever he did – and I'm not sure I was ever told the full extent of the incident – it worked a treat.

The evening for the first puppy training class arrives at last. They are weekly sessions, scheduled to take place over a period of two months. My rollercoaster hopes are soaring. Not only am I a Dog Owner In Need of Help, there is something of the class swot about me. I can't wait to be told and shown what to do. I am also certain that residing in Mabel's poodle head is a great deal of intelligence. All it needs is pointing in the right direction.

The venue, a church hall, is a fifteen-minute journey away and Mabel has outgrown her car coffin. Since she is still too small and wild to be let loose in the car, I have bought a harness which cleverly attaches to a seat belt. I use it to strap her into the passenger seat, bracing myself for tantrums.

To my astonishment, she submits meekly. So meekly, I even pause to wonder if she is unwell. She doesn't look unwell. She looks regal, sitting up staring thoughtfully and calmly ahead as we set off, almost as if life with me – side by side as equals – is finally delivering the standards she expected of it. She maintains this serene pose the entire way, apart from shooting me the occasional glance, as if to say, you've clocked those bollards up on the left, haven't you, and I think we both know you didn't mean to shoot that yellow light.

By the time we pull up outside the church hall my puppy love has skyrocketed to new heights. This is exactly the doggy companionship I dreamed of. Mabel and me, pootling around town. Side by side. In harmony. Bezzie mates for life. A corner has been turned. A distant memory surfaces of a great-aunt called Joanie. As children we had a lot of great-aunts and were forced to visit them when on home leave, often packing several into one day. Aunt-upping, we called it. Our main job as youngsters was to eat whatever was put in front of us, and by the end of a twelve-hour marathon of elevenses, lunch, tea and dinner, comprising all sorts of things beyond our usual diets, some of them disgusting, we were staggering under the discomfort of our protesting digestive systems.

Aunt Joanie was always my favourite because she had a dog, a dear little bouncy black curly haired creature who went everywhere with her, including in the car, often on her lap, much to the detriment of her already wobbly driving and the amused horror of my parents. The dog's name escapes me now, but it was a labradoodle. I remember the fondness with which Mum said the word – the first time I ever heard it – and the hint of envy in her tone, the Moojik years being still a distant dream. I marvel at how the Great-Aunt Joanie memory should be surfacing now, rising like flotsam after five decades of burial. I love to think how my subconscious must have held it and cherished it all those years, needing the right triggers to set it free: a dog. A car. A solitary old lady. Me.

★

The bumph circulated in advance of the class has made it plain that the methods to be deployed are based on rewarding obedience with treats. Secretly I am sceptical. Surely a dog should behave out of a desire to please rather than the desire to gobble food? Nevertheless, I have packed a handful of treats, as instructed, as well as a couple of Mabel's favourite toys, just in case she needs distracting. On entering the hall, which has been neatly laid out with six mats, six water bowls and six chairs (for the owners), my first thought is of how similar it looks to my Pilates class. It is not a thought that stays with me for long.

The state of zen tranquillity Mabel had managed for the journey evaporates in an instant. She has never seen six dogs together in such close confines. She cannot believe her luck. She thinks I have brought her to a doggy disco. She strains to be released from her lead like a tethered wild pony. And she barks. And barks and barks and barks. The other animals soon settle, curling on their mats at their owners' feet, lapping at their water, chewing on their chew toys. Mabel wants

119

to do none of these things. She capsizes her water bowl, scrabbles her mat into a knot and ignores her toys. And she continues to bark. All she wants is to play with the other dogs. She thinks that if she makes a sufficiently voluble protest this wish will be granted. The hall has high ceilings, perfect for the reverberation of sound. I am powerless (my new default state), embarrassed, deeply disappointed and sorely tempted to leave.

The teacher is sweet. She talks louder – over the sound of Mabel – and says barking is normal. After ten minutes, when Mabel is still making it impossible for anyone to hear anything, she goes to her car and fetches a much more interesting toy for Mabel to play with. Mabel loves this toy. She stops barking. Unfortunately it is the noisiest dog toy ever invented – a rattling, crackling one – and the audibility of our guru's instructions remains a challenge. I can feel the impatience from my fellow attendees mounting, radiating like heat-waves towards our corner of the hall. I don't blame them. They have busy lives and dogs to train. They have paid good money to be here. Mabel, meanwhile, is tossing her new rattling toy in the air like a professional juggler, hurling herself onto it when it lands and then shaking it violently before the next toss. She is the Show-Off pain in the neck, wanting everyone to look. She is sabotaging the class.

After a few minutes the teacher approaches our mat again. This time Mabel goes bonkers. She has decided she loves this woman. Owner of exciting rattling toys and multiple doggy scents, she is, literally, the most exciting person she has ever met. Mabel has decided she wants to stay as close to her as she can. On top of her, preferably.

I try and fail to calm Mabel down. She rears up, yanking against the lead. She barks. I grit my teeth, expecting a quiet, tactful expulsion from the proceedings. We are a disruptive influence. We are ruining the education of others. If the teacher had given me a dunce's hat I would have put it on.

'Try this,' she says instead. She hands me a slab of something she describes as 'liver cake', clearly homemade. I accept it gratefully. My earlier scepticism about treats is already a distant memory. Food. Drugs. Whipping. I would try anything to shut up my baying hound. I give Mabel a morsel of the cake, and a look of discernible surprise and pleasure suffuses her doggy chops as she chomps. Without being asked, she immediately sits, 'begging' for another. And I oblige. Her silence is blissful. I never want it to end.

Over the course of the next hour, between, during and after the various exercises, I drip-feed Mabel the entire slab of this magical food, regardless of whether she has done anything to deserve it. As we are leaving, I stop by the teacher, both to apologize for the disruption we caused and to ask for the recipe. During this fresh encounter Mabel's love for our instructor reaches a new fever pitch. She wants to stay with her. Forever. Not even the liver cake surpasses her love for this woman. I end up having to drag her away, feeling not unlike a guard frogmarching a prisoner back to Colditz.

The moment we reach the car, however, Mabel hops onto the front passenger seat and assumes her tranquil 'Drive on, Jeeves' pose, nose in the air, as if nothing has happened. As if all we have been doing for the last hour and a half is strolling round the block, kicking up the drifts of soggy leaves. If there were crowds lining the streets she would wave a paw. For my own part, I find I am incapable of making so sudden a switch. I am still in a stew. So much so that as soon as I am seated next to her I start to shout, letting all my grievances pour out. How she has let me down. How she can move in with the teacher and see if I care. How I am not paying for puppy training just so she can gorge herself on liver cake. How if she thinks I am going to start baking her homemade treats she has got another think coming. Mabel remains demure throughout the dressing-down. When finally I turn the engine on, she emits a long sigh and settles down to sleep, as if she is the one having to put up with me rather than the other way round.

Back home Tiger Lily breaks all protocol and is waiting in the hall to greet us. My volatile emotions swoop back upwards. She and Mabel even manage a nose-nuzzle before Mabel ruins it by doing one of her let's-play bunnyhops. I pour a large glass of wine, put the telly on and collapse on the sofa. Mabel jumps up to join me, stretching out on her faux-fur rug (the best of my dog-investments by a mile) with her head on my lap and doing that thing of showing her teeth, which looks like a grin but can't be because she is a dog.

'Sorry, sweetie,' I say, stroking her lovely silky head and feeling how it softens as she relaxes under my hand. 'Sorry for losing it in the car.'

On the telly two bears lope into view. It's David Attenborough. Mabel sits up, studying them intently, her nose twitching as she tries to work out what they are. When the bears start to fight she scrambles onto my lap, making the Scooby Doo noises she reserves for objects of deepest suspicion (helicopters, kites, flapping plastic bags). As the fight intensifies she presses against me, eventually burying her head under my arm. Glancing across the room, I see that Tiger Lily, perched on her usual chair-back, is equally spellbound, whisking her leopard tail, her eyes hunting-black and fixed upon the screen. When a pod of jumping orca whales suddenly replaces the bears, both pets do a double take. Mabel slides off my lap and goes to sit directly in front of the telly, wagging her tail as she watches the great fish move. Behind her, Tiger Lily too has sat up so she can get a better view. Happiness washes through me. Oh lord. Watching TV with my little crew. The ridiculous joy of it.

I am falling in love with my dog. It is a new love, this. A different sort of love. A simple one, built on supply and demand. I give Mabel what she needs – food, protection, affection, exercise – and in return she, mostly, shows a preference for my company, with the added bonus of keeping me fit and (between bouts of mortification) making me laugh. Trust is at the heart of it, just as in the best relationships between humans. But again it is a simpler, surer trust, because animals have no words to hide behind. They cannot exaggerate their faith or fake it. It is there or it isn't. It has to be earned, through action. You know where you stand.

I have no idea if Mabel 'loves' me in return. She is certainly growing used to me. And happily, with animals, familiarity breeds loyalty rather than contempt. Yay. Happily too, she cannot feel the neediness in me, how I hold her too close. She does not know she is helping to heal a wound. If a few tears fall into her fur she doesn't notice. Once, when a black wave hits unexpectedly, as they do – a too-quiet room, the aloneness stretching ahead, the visceral stab of what has been lost – I start to cry properly and she comes to my side. I think, like my singing, it is the sound that alarms her more than anything. I reach out to stroke her and feel comforted, but still desolate. It helps to have her there. But it was never my plan in life to have an animal rather than a human at my side.

We anthropomorphize our pets because it suits us to do so. It makes us happy. We give them human names and cuddle them. We tell them they are 'naughty' or 'good' or 'grumpy'. All of it is simply a reflection of that terrible need we have in ourselves, to love and be loved in return.

At the next class Mabel behaves fractionally better. Her owner is less stressed, which almost certainly helps. Like children, dogs are sponges, soaking up mood and atmosphere. I also have liver cake. Lashings of it. Made by me, of course – who was I kidding? The show-off in her is also starting to enjoy the actual training exercises, often done while other members of the class watch. She prances like Spot the Dog at my side, staring at me lovingly because she knows of the treat in store. She does her doggy grin; she licks her lips. It starts to dawn on me how much she loves knowing what is expected of her. It is uncertainty that makes her bark. Best of all is the growing realization that whatever Mabel's 'feelings' are for me, they are not the key to ensnaring her co-operation. People I have loved may have rejected me, but with Mabel no such emotions are at stake. Training a dog is like mathematics. Pavlov was spot on. Dogs do things through learned responses. Bells. Words. Treats. Whistles. Clickers. Whatever works. It's all about programming. Reward a 'correct' behaviour and it is more likely to be repeated. The real trick is getting the timing right, because dogs live so in the moment. A few seconds too early or late can make all the difference. A dog must never be muddled as to why it is being praised.

I love all my new doggy knowledge. I take Mabel into the park with fresh courage. I abandon the horrible training lead which trips us up and ties us in cat's cradles. I take toys instead to make being with me more fun. I may not cut a dash, weighed down by whistles, treats, balls, strings of plastic sausages, and squeaky duck toys, but we start to make progress. There is the sound of authority in my commands instead of wild hope. Mabel hears it too.

For all the irresistible parallels between dog ownership and parenthood, I start to see that training a dog is the opposite of bringing up a child. It is my duty to make Mabel as dependent on me as it is possible to be. Forever. Never will the day arrive when the pair of us can have a heart-to-heart about the dangers of getting into a white van with a stranger, even one waggling slabs of steak. Never will I be able to warn her about the poisonous algae shimmering in the pond near our house into which she longs, every day, to dive headlong. Never will I get the chance to point out that chasing a squirrel across the South Circular is likely to result in death, hers being the least of it. No milestone moment will come when I wave her off through misty eyes at an airport or bus station, having performed a last-minute check for vital travel documents and blister packs of malaria tablets. Mabel is an innocent who will always need my protection. I am responsible for every single thing she does. She has her rights, but I own her. She is mine.

In the human world no one owns anybody. Our children belong to us only as gifts, needing to pass through the transit of our care. You equip them to leave you. Parents who do not do this are failing in their duty. Independence is the greatest blessing we can bestow.

Between adults, the highest demonstration of love we can perform is to give each other freedom, to choose what we do and to be ourselves. To say 'I am yours' to another person should be voluntary, a matter of self-appointment. No one has the right to demand the endearment. No person possesses another person. Any attempt to enforce the concept is poison to a relationship. It is the language of bullies.

★

When Mum first found God we worried for Dad. He had always been Number One and now there was a rival. And quite a formidable rival too. Mum was suddenly in church all the time, or reading from her bible, or abdicating from the intellectual arguments she had once enjoyed, offering up – sometimes maddeningly – panacea answers along the lines of the Lord being in charge of everything. Dad did not bat an eye. A staunch atheist with a rapier brain, he could have eviscerated her, but he did the opposite. He let her be. He respected every word she said. He did not mock. He did not judge. He did not grill. And when the early years of the fervour subsided, just as any fervour will, no matter to whom or to what it is directed, he made no remark or interrogation then either, beyond what Mum herself sought in the process of trying to make sense of it. No couple I have ever known were so beautifully together and so beautifully separate. It was wonderful to witness, but hard to live up to. Impossible, as it turned out.

⋆

A man is coming to dinner. Platonically. But still. He is a friend of friends, someone I know slightly. He is divorced, single, affluent, eligible. The dog-owner chic won't do. I must up my game. I get a haircut. I use a face pack. I try extra hard at brushing my teeth. I buy nice food. I scrub the kitchen floor. On the day itself I walk Mabel again and again. I need her exhausted, in the land of Nod, so that this man and I can talk about matters worldly and scintillating. Uncertainty claws at my innards. I don't feel scintillating. I have to remind myself that a million years ago I was someone who could have breezed a date like this. That I can be that person again.

The man arrives just as I am getting back from walking Mabel round the block for the hundredth time. It is dark and a light rain is falling. I have the very large hood of my (new) anorak up in a bid to protect my recently coiffed hair. This causes the far from ideal opening moment of not being recognized. I am simply a woman in the street in an unglamorous coat whose dog is jumping up at him, wiping her wet black paws on his clean trousers.

All the hellos turn into apologies. 'She'll calm down,' I assure him. 'She's always like this with strangers, especially men.' Aware that this might sound as if I am constantly in the company of male strangers, I hurry us inside, where Mabel does the opposite of calming down. Do I regret getting a dog? he asks, while I alternate between attempts to offer him a drink and undertaking a worse-than-usual fight with Mabel and the smelly towel responsible for drying her paws. No, I answer, suspecting that he is the one already harbour-ing regrets about my dog ownership and acutely aware that whatever flimsy allure to which I might have laid claim is already in tatters. My Chanel No. 19 is overlaid by damp dog. My hair is messed up. I have dirty smears on my clothes, as does my visitor. Mabel is dominating everything, mucking up everything. Literally.

I direct him to a bottle of champagne so I can continue to sort out my hound, and things start to look up. Mabel settles at last and we eat at the kitchen table, racing through topics like speed-daters: books, plays, families, countries visited, foods preferred. It feels like we are interviewing each other, albeit very enjoyably. When the meal is done we retreat to a Mabel-free room to finish the champagne. We sit like the new acquaintances we are, but agree it might be nice to meet again. There *is* a game, I tell myself, and I can be in it if I want to. I just need to hold my nerve. Take it step by step. Not rush. I have no idea what I think about this man. Getting to know someone new was never going to be easy. Not for him either, I am sure. After a certain age there is so much baggage to be factored in, on both sides. It takes effort, time.

He says he must be on his way and I lead us back to the kitchen where he has left his coat. All is quiet and I open the door with confidence. I am greeted by the grimmest of spectacles: lakes of dark brown diarrhoea everywhere and Mabel skipping excitedly through them to say hello. I am too appalled to be worried whether she is ill.

She doesn't look remotely ill. I am also a little too full of champagne and wine to think straight. Squawking my horror and apologies at my guest, I hurl Mabel into the garden and start scrambling for kitchen paper and mops and buckets. The man nobly delays his departure, offering to keep an eye on Mabel outside while I clear up. He laughs, as do I. There is not a lot else to do.

When I join him in the drizzle, zipped back up in my anorak, hands scrubbed, he asks me with schoolboy eagerness if I happen to have any cigarettes, and I say I have given up. So have I, he confesses, gleefully. No, I explain, over-earnest, I really have given up. Ten years ago. I will never have another cigarette in my life. I get an inkling of having ruined a moment. He wants someone to be bad with, to break rules with. I might have been that someone once, but not anymore.

It is obvious the evening could have gone better, but I feel a sort of pride at having managed it at all. We liked each other, and that is something. We have also agreed to meet again, before too long. We part as platonically as we met. A kiss on the cheek. A lukewarm farewell. I know desire and there is no hint of it here. But I have been mauled by love. Savaged. And lukewarm suits me just fine.

7

Boxing the Past

I am driving south to my mother's house. For the first time, Mabel, at the grand old age of four months, has been promoted (or relegated perhaps, in her view), sans harness, to the backseat. To my relief, she maintains her newfound car-calmness, at first attempting to stay sitting – she likes to watch the road ahead – but eventually giving up and lying down. I am sort of glad that there is no way of explaining to her that we are not on a ten-minute jaunt as usual but undertaking a journey which, on a bad day, can take over two hours. Doggy happiness is so much about having no clue of what is to come.

The route, used over decades, is achingly familiar:

the stretch of motorway, the endless roundabouts, the winding country lanes. Once the entire drive felt like a meander in the countryside; now it is more like patches of green between concrete. Only the last bit is still truly rural: the same trees lining the way, taller, thicker, darker, like the vaulting walls of a cathedral; the same potholed road for the final mile, crumbling as always, but worse than I have ever known it after the deluges of autumn. My car, a townie like its owner, beeps and skids and struggles.

My siblings are heading in the same direction. There is to be a gathering of the four of us, the first in a while. The plan is to start, at last, to go through some of the contents of the house. Thanks to the tireless vigilance of the elder sister who lives nearby, the place has now been kept in a holding pattern for longer than any of us care to think about too closely. The grass gets cut, fresh flowers occupy vases on the windowsills, curtains are drawn and opened, the radio and TV hum, lights flick on and off at pre-set hours. It is a system designed both to deter intruders and to give us the time we need to resolve our discussions.

So much time. We never dreamed how much. It has kept the lawyers shamefully busy while Mum's empty home continues to bear testimony to the stasis. Once the vibrant nucleus of the family, the house is now more akin to a creature on life support: all the carefully managed outward indicators of existence somehow only serving to emphasize the essence of life that is lacking. It makes arriving hard. All the myriad loved things – the crunch of gravel under my car wheels as I pull into the drive, the duck pond, the sag of the camellias clinging to the wall, the warp on the front gate – are the same, and yet so utterly changed. Sic transit gloria mundi indeed.

Going inside is even worse. The smell is the same. The house is the same. The telly is on, as it always was, but Mum's chair is empty.

I am the first to arrive. I have paid several visits since Mum's death, but this is my first with Mabel. Her delight at being released from the car is explosive. After a long pee by the empty duck pond, she races inside, exploring corners, sniffing greedily at the furniture, the cushions, the carpets. She must smell traces of Mum, I realize, liking the thought; and Lucky, of course, Mum's last dog, not to mention Bentley, the quirky last cat, long since adopted by a willing niece. To my pooch there is no poignancy, no nostalgia, no if-onlys. It is simply a big fresh exciting world. New smells, new space.

Mabel is even more elated by the garden. She hurtles round the molehills on the lawn, past the wonky white bench where Dad used to sit, enjoying the view after a session with the mower, his weathered face strong and calm behind the fuzz of his cigarette smoke; she dives in and out of the mass of rhododendrons that my mother so loved, (calling them, always, purely for her own amusement, *ro-dun-den-drons*); she tunnels through the blue sea of lavender skirting the rose bushes, before braking to a comically abrupt halt in front of the small rectangular fish pool that sits in the lee of a crumbling old sundial. Under the water the goldfish teem. Mabel is spellbound. In fact the pond is sorely overpopulated, yet one more tugging indicator of the house's emptiness, its lack of a chatelaine. Mabel trembles with longing. She is half waterdog. She has webbed paws. She yearns to belly-flop into and play among the slithery shoal. Fortunately there is a cover of strong mesh to deter her, an ancient measure put in place by my father against mishaps with toddling grandchildren.

As Mabel and I continue our circuit I am aware that my usual post-Mum sadness is thinner, lighter. It is a fine, bright winter day. The views, rolling in green waves towards the great distant velvety-grey wall of the South Downs are as breathtaking as they have ever been. They are one of the reasons the lawyers are earning money. We don't want to sell this place. In the absence of specific instructions from Mum, the ongoing struggle is about finding a way – a fair, affordable way that we all agree on – of keeping it in the family. The house itself, of red brick with white windows and terracotta roof tiles, is far from grand, and sorely in need of refurbishment. But it has been a part of our lives forever. It came into being not from any silver spoons in mouths but because of a great-grandfather who walked into a brick factory aged fourteen and asked for a job. It was where Mum grew up, as did her father before her.

Sometimes, when I am far away, I can convince myself it is only bricks and mortar and that all the lawyer stuff is a lot of fuss about nothing. But every time I visit I know that it isn't. Quite apart from the spectacular location, the house has a warmth that speaks uniquely to us. Its scratches and dents, ingrained and painted over across the years, are like the faint etchings of a private fossil. For four generations its mossy old walls have circled hopes and losses, played host to countless wakes and celebrations. They have held firm while the outside world raged and raced ever onwards, tumbling the family in its wake. It may be a place on life support but there is breath in it still. To give up and sell without a fight would feel like surrendering a chunk of ourselves.

At the sound of the gravel crunching under another set of car wheels, my heart tightens. Under any circumstances what the four of us are about to do would be hard: the divvying up, the dividing, knick-knack by knick-knack, picture by picture, book by book, letter by letter, of not just our parents' lives, but so much of our own. Eeeny meeny miny moe. Parcelling out cherished mementoes like counters in a game. Familiar musky scents will assail us as we open drawers. Round every corner the cudgel of memories lurks, in each ornament, each photo, each shoe; in the faded designs on Mum's favourite overwashed tea mugs; in the carefully folded support stockings which she so loathed, stacked neatly on a shelf in the airing cupboard. In her coat pockets there will be old tissues, stiff from use. Inside her beloved hats, lined like trophies along the pegs above the wellington boots, will be silver spools of her long fine hair. She was proud of her hair. She hated anyone to touch it. She brushed it every night, literally, to her dying day, rhythmically, religiously, assiduously, exactly as she had been taught to as a child.

The shadow being cast by the lawyers' discussions makes everything harder still. There have been some difficult conversations. Abandoned options. Tensions.

★

It was E.M. Forster who lured me into literature. I was sixteen and, though relatively well read, had never fallen in love with a story until I opened *Howards End*. He had me at the opening line. *One may as well begin with Helen's letters to her sister.* So laid-back. So in control. So beguiling. Never before had I encountered a book that managed to combine page-turning entertainment with such tender, wise and wryly funny observations on the world. By the end I felt I understood myself better, as well as everyone around me.

Howards End is, among many other things, a book about a house. A house that draws people together and pulls them apart. A house with a spirit, an *essence*. A house that demands its rightful inheritor and somehow gets her, against all odds. There is one particular scene which I have always loved, when after months of estrangement the two sisters, Helen and Margaret, are reunited by finding themselves inside Howards End and surrounded by (thanks to a series of unplanned, fortuitous crossed wires) all the possessions of their childhood. The two women have been at such a distance for so long and yet, conversing among these familiar, beloved objects – the jigsaw of their shared past – all their differences gradually dissolve.

And so it is with the four of us on this winter day. We hug our hellos, we roll up our sleeves, we make a start. Room by room. Cupboard by cupboard. Trinket by trinket. We move together, a pack of four, the same pack who learned to be each other's best friends on far-flung postings round the world. We fill bags and boxes. We laugh and we shed tears. Chip by chip we chisel at our huge task. It will take more visits, but we know this first matters most, that it sets the tone. We are methodical, fair, and, at times, absurdly generous to one another. 'No, you have that because I know how much it means to you.' That sort of thing. It is sublime. It is the best of all of us, coming together, combining forces just as our parents had always taught us we should.

We break for lunch, a makeshift meal, cobbled together with what we have each managed to pull out of our own fridges. Chicken, ham, bread, salad. Someone fetches some sprigs of fresh mint and basil from the bed by the back door. We catch up on other matters as we eat. Children. Jobs. My Diarrhoea Date. It is wonderful to make them all laugh again, especially about so potentially a delicate subject as a possible new suitor. I realize that my meltdown is fast becoming a mere memory to them, just as I hope it will one day be for me. They do not need to hear how it rises up sometimes, a demon in the dark. I am managing. Bearing instead of buckling. Fixing my colours to the mast of Mabel. Looking ahead.

We don't stop again until the darkening afternoon signals that it is time to walk the dogs, three all told. The day has grown icy. We deck ourselves out in an assortment of the outdoor gear from the utility room, us girls in old anoraks, hats, scarves and boots of Mum's, the brother in a cap and coat of Dad's. His resemblance to our father is so strong that I have to look away. And the echoes of Mum in my sisters is also uncanny, the shape of their mouths, the set of their eyes, the way they hold their heads as they talk and move. We make a motley crew, orphans attired in patchwork pieces of their parents, talking quietly as we stride through the gloaming, the dogs bounding at our heels. As the smallest of the four (hence my father's nickname for me of 'Small'), Mum's clothes fit me the worst: the sleeves of her anorak flap over my hands and my feet paddle in her size-seven boots, but I am both warm and profoundly aware of a comfort that reaches beyond the science of thick clothing. Grief is indeed like fear, and we are conquering ours.

All day Mabel has been like the new kid on the block with my sisters' two older dogs, belting round in circles to get their attention, copying what they do, idolizing, trying too hard like the ninny-no-mates she is. On the walk she goes berserk with showing off, bouncing after them through the castles of dead bracken like a jack-in-the-box and madly digging holes when we reach the inviting sandy pathway that leads up to the trig point. Once there, she collapses panting as we pause – as all of us always have – to drink in the view that never fails to astound, across the common towards the soft wending wall of the Downs. The silver birches shimmer in the dying light; the last mercury-blue slants of sun catch the mint green of the fields. None of us want to leave, but quite suddenly it is dark. The sisters' dogs, both black, are hard to spot as we pick our way back down towards the house. Only Mabel, with her milky-white coat, continues to shine, impossible to lose, a zigzagging star shooting through the shadows. I watch her with a full heart. I cannot believe she is mine. I cannot believe I get to take her home.

Fiction can magnify life, make it worse or better. It can play tricks with time and grant wishes. It can tie up loose ends and open secret worlds. It can give us endings and beginnings, shape lines through the chaos of our daily lives. But sometimes – occasionally – reality can deliver moments just as perfect; moments when everything, fleetingly, comes together in a magical fusion of people, place and mood. So it was for the four of us that day. It was as if Time itself coiled up and held its breath, granting us a space in which we could simply be.

We were our parents' children again. Nothing else mattered but our connection to them and our love.

Back in London Mabel sets about reminding me that she isn't a shooting star, she's a growing, naughty puppy. Perhaps inspired by the soft Sussex sand, she resumes her favourite pastime of massacring the lawn with renewed vigour. The damage is so bad, the holes she digs so deep, that I resort to filling them with stones and placing planks over them, a desperate remedy that makes the garden look like a builder's yard and which serves only to encourage her to mine new areas.

She also ups her game in terms of trying to engage with Tiger Lily, displaying a new brute enthusiasm and cunning that I fear might become the norm; every twitch and Mabel is onto my poor moggy, pouncing, chasing, cornering. I yell, so loudly I sear my throat. Mabel always stops instantly, the picture of meekness and remorse, and then does it again at the next opportunity. Her fragile confidence back in tatters, Tiger Lily starts to spend more and more time upstairs, where Mabel is Absolutely Forbidden To Go. But Mabel begins to try her luck there too, deploying the sly tactic of stretching herself in a show of sleepy indifference, draught-excluder style, along the bottom of the staircase and then tiptoeing upwards, step by step, the moment my back is turned. Tiptoeing is the only word. It is a sight to behold. A sight that makes me want to laugh out loud, because it is so sweetly done, and because she freezes mid-tiptoe the moment she realizes I am looking, as if trying to convert her crime into a game of Grandmother's Footsteps. Sometimes, if I don't happen to catch her en route, I stumble across her upstairs, in corners and behind doors, curled as tight as can be, her head under her paws, following that delightful animal and baby logic that not being able to see means there is no danger of being seen.

Oh lord, she is so cute. So scrumptious. I want to give in. Every time. I have to grit my teeth, picture the paw prints on my new stair carpets, the smelly nest she'd make of my duvet, the trauma such freedom would pose to the already traumatized Tiger Lily. So instead I growl, 'Downstairs,' in my best Top Dog voice. I look as grim as can be. One hint of a smile and I know I'm a goner. Like kids, dogs are alert to every chink in your armour. Mabel never makes it easy. Her tail droops like a flag down a pole. Her chocolate eyes flood with suffering. Her head hangs in mourning. Oh yes, the phrase 'hangdog' came into being for good reason.

With kids you can say, okay, just for today. But a dog needs one set of rules. Exceptions will only confuse it. Mabel, castigated, slopes back down to the TV room and curls up on her faux-fur rug on the sofa. Diddums! I still feel like a monster. I slink after her, prepared to be ignored or punished for my cruelty. But Mabel is merely thrilled to find me nearby. She rolls onto her back for a tummy rub. She knows nothing about punishment or grudges. She's all about the now-ness of now, and that's the joy of her.

We are definitely in a new phase though. One night she suddenly refuses to enter her cage, even when I pat the tatty gold cushion and command her to. Seventy-odd nights of going in, and suddenly she won't. It's a big crate too, so it's not about the size. She sits on the kitchen floor instead, looking between me and the metal door as if I have taken leave of my senses. I experience an onrush of the old panic. I had some control and now it is going. She is on to me, has found out my fragility, is realizing her true power. The same week she stops coming when I call during our walks, throwing a casual glance over her shoulder instead before resuming whatever it is that interests her more: chasing another dog, eating a discarded slab of pizza, paddling in a puddle, staking out a pigeon. She is gaining in confidence. Life is opening up, introducing new menus of possibilities, and I am getting in the way of them.

Change can be hard. The need to adapt our systems. It makes us afraid. One evening, reading to my sons, as I had every night for over a decade, a treasured pocket of peace at the end of each hectic day, I suddenly realized that their attention to the story-telling was partly to please me. They liked being read to, but they were also factoring in my wants. A balance had shifted. I hadn't seen it, hadn't wanted to see it. They were growing up, becoming more self-aware, more separate, as children must if they are to thrive.

Only a couple of years later my eldest put an arm round me to pull me back off a busy road. We had just bought him new football boots and were returning to the car. A lorry thundered past, inches from my toes. I said thank you as we tried again, making it to the other side. This time I held his hand, newly aware of how he was holding mine.

The carload of boxes lugged back from the grand sort-out in Sussex continues to sit in the hall. I clean and hoover round them. I shove at them. They make me feel bad. Filling them was hard enough, but now emptying them feels impossible. I dread the flocks of memories sealed inside, waiting to fly at me all over again, stirring up all the emotions I am trying to leave behind. Nor do I relish the labour of decision-making that will unfold: finding shelf spaces for the ornaments and books, cupboard spaces for the crockery; picture-hooks for the pictures, not to mention a hammer and the certainty about where to bang it. Few tasks highlight the challenge of living alone so effectively as the need to hang a picture.

But one Sunday I stumble in from a walk with Mabel, and the riptides of sadness are circling any-way. The house is too empty and too dark, and Mabel has been a tearaway terror, chasing a dog out of the park and onto the road. That there hap-pened to be no cars passing at the time was little consolation. I flick the hall light on and the stack of boxes glares at me, blocking my way. I feel I am in danger of stalling again, as a dog owner, as a person.

Each box is very heavy. A son had helped me transfer them from the car to the hall. Wary of my ever-problematic back, I now manhandle the easiest to reach onto a table. Mabel, hopeful of some new entertainment, parks herself in a corner, watching. The box is one of the ones from my childhood bedroom, easy and speedy to fill since there were no debates about ownership or custody of the contents.

I open the flaps, and there, perched on top though I have no recollection of placing it there, is a tiny little book that I recognize with a jolt, the same jolt I had experienced as a ten-year-old, plucking it out of the heel of my Christmas stocking. It is a diary, the first thrilling invitation I had ever received to put pen – actually a tiny pencil, slotted into the spine – to paper outside of a classroom. Better still, to my ten-year-old eyes, it proudly declared itself a *Dog Owner's Diary*, a point demonstrated by a jacket photo of a glorious toffee-coloured hound which I can remember – as if it were yesterday – instantly longing to possess. In real life I was as far from being a dog owner as it is possible to be. We were between postings to Germany and Sweden. The acquisition of the great Mooge was years off, not even a pipe dream.

I have to sit down at the table. I cannot believe I had forgotten not just this little gem, but the intensity of the childhood passion that had made it so special. Few gifts (truly) have made me happier. Other memories swoop in. As a little girl I had wanted to be a 'kennel maid' – for years that had been my stock answer to any inquiry about future plans. I had got the term from my mother, asking her one day what you called a person who worked with dogs and delighting that there was an actual answer.

I leaf through the diary tenderly. It dawns on me the extent to which this tiny book probably unlocked my desire to be a writer: its mini pages are crammed with my girlish spidery scrawl – what I had eaten for breakfast, whether I was happy, which friend or sibling had done me wrong. Between the entries are numerous other scribblings, including drawings of dogs, helpfully labelled with arrows to their body parts – 'ear', 'leg', 'nose' (I clearly had little faith in my abilities as a graphic artist, but actually there is one of a Dalmatian that really isn't bad) – and a series of earnest declarations reflecting the seriousness of my doggy ardour:

Prayer For Dogs: Dear God, please help all the stray dogs in the world and bless those that have died of starvation. And make all happy dogs grateful. Help us to be kind to all animals throughout our whole lives. Amen.

VOW: I solemnly vow to love and care for all dogs during my whole life.

RESOLUTION: To own a lovely large well-groomed dog, take it to shows and win prizes. It shall be well trained and liked by everyone that I know. PS Look after my parents.

The PS makes me hoot. Oh, the guilt of loving dogs more than my parents! What imaginary audience had I thought I would be fooling with such a postscript? And how irresistible to decide that here, already, was the latent writer in me, grappling with the unavoidable and exciting fact that all written matter can only ever be a version of truth: history, journalism, fiction, biography, memoirs – it makes no difference; all they can offer are angles of reflection, myriad sides of a prism, each one ineluctably linked to the inner life of their creators.

Mabel, woken from her snoozing by my chortles, is sitting up, looking concerned. I stroke her dear bemused shaggy face, marvelling that I could have lost touch so completely with the fervour of my girlhood yearning to possess exactly such a creature. I get on the floor for a roll-around, just to reassure her that all is well. More than well. We do our usual silly wrestling-tickling, the trauma of her life-threatening disobedience in the park forgotten. And as we play I decide I will order a book specifically about dog recall that one of my best doggy friends has been recommending for weeks. Apparently all you need is a special sort of whistle and some fresh chicken. How hard can that be?

Sensing my new high spirits, Mabel lollops off to fetch her favourite tug-of-war toy and we carry on playing till my arms ache. It dawns on me that the reason I want her to learn always to come when I call is not because I am a control freak, but because I love her. We may not be able to stop the people we care about from leaving us, but if I am to lose Mabel, it shall not be for want of doing my utmost to keep her safe and by my side.

On the table above us, the handsome dog on the jacket of my Dog Owner's Diary (still the sole product of my unpacking) gleams under the beam of the table lamp, back in the spotlight after forty-six years of invisibility. I had thought Mabel was a new idea, but she was an old one. She had been there all along, waiting to come into being.

Emptying the boxes properly takes several days and is nothing like the burden I had anticipated. It turns out the flocks of memories are becoming old friends, just like the objects themselves. I experience a tingle of pleasure every time I catch sight of them in their new allocated homes – the iridescent Swedish blue stone reindeer on the kitchen windowsill, the small Chinese jade plate sitting next to a recent beach photo of my sons, the print of St George slaying the dragon on the wall beside my bed, keeping a watchful eye just as it did over a kitchen table in my teens. They are threads of my past, knitting with the present, just as they should.

One day I seize one of the empty boxes and fill it with all the things that remind me of the man. I sellotape the flaps shut and write across them in bold black felt pen: *In the event of my death burn without opening.* My feelings for him might dim with time, but I cannot – and have no wish to – alter or undo them. Love, the real kind, does not end because the loved one has gone, in whatever form that departure might have taken. Love has its own tense. It just is. That is why it is so mighty.

I hide the sellotaped box behind some old suitcases. It contains nothing that I want anyone else to see. Its existence is purely, for me, a last physical link to what I cannot yet let go. It feels good to close the door on it though. I walk away better, lighter. Safer. I know I have the kind of family who would honour a message scrawled on a box lid. I have no doubts about this. They are simply that sort. Every last one of them. I realize both how lucky that makes me, and that feeling lucky and feeling happy are pretty hard to tell apart.

8

Health & Beauty

I am developing serious calf muscles. My 'new' wellies, used so much, split along the soles and need to be replaced. One day the younger son, with the usual eye-roll of despair at his mother's techno-ignorance, shows me the inbuilt app on my phone that records how many steps I am taking a day. To be fit, you are supposed to do 10,000. I am averaging 18,000, and that doesn't include going up and down my long staircase and squeezing in the occasional jog. I realize that some nights I am sleeping better than I have done in a very long while and that my daily lunchtime tussles with the *Times* crossword are resolving at unprecedented speeds. I despatch three meals a day and still my jeans hang looser. I am also starting to sing again, not just rehearsing with my choir, but in the car and round the house. One evening I sit at the piano and manage to push out the words of the 'Ave Maria' which the dear niece had performed so exquisitely at Mum's funeral. The sounds I make are laughably far from exquisite, but I make it to the end for the first time.

Tentatively, between walks and playing tug-of-war games, I start to venture upstairs for short bursts at my desk. The still unpublished novel is beginning to feel comfortably distant, a child that will find its own place in the light, when the time is right. It is a story I wanted to tell. I am proud of it. Meanwhile I can feel the desire to write thrumming again, a pulse inside. It is like glimpsing a lost love. The subject for a new project remains out of focus, and I know better than to thrash around looking for it. Instead I jot random ideas in my many notebooks: Big Thoughts, little thoughts, character sketches, nuggets for short stories, funny Mabel moments. It is called fiddling. It is what writers do. Often for me it is about taking pleasure in the act of writing itself, the fetish kick of good stationery – the softness of a Moleskine jacket under one's palms, the slide of the ink filling a clean white page, the faint, lovely resistance of the pen nib as it moves against the grain. It is creative faffing, pre-paratory feathering, a sign that a new reproductive cycle might be about to begin. I had forgotten all about this, the sheer bliss of it.

Something extraordinary is happening to Mabel. Six months old now and her hair won't stop grow-ing. All the cute tufty puppy kinks have gone. In their place is an ever-lengthening, ever-thickening dense, curly, snowy verdure of fluffy fronds. She is like some canine leylandii bush; every time I look she is more bearded, more voluptuous, more Dougal-from-the-Magic-Roundabout. Her paws have become luxury slippers. When she runs, her whole coat ripples in the manner of a field of wheat in a high wind. Like one of those adverts for healthy living. Cruella de Vil would be sharpening her knives.

She's suddenly really got the hang of running too. No more the puppy lollop. Instead, arriving overnight it seems, is a proper dog-gallop, all four paws at full stretch as she pelts across the park, pursuing playmates, squirrels, balls or someone she likes the look of. It is a thing of beauty to behold, particularly with the rippling hair thing going on. People stop us even more than when she was diddy and sweet. They want to touch her Farrah Fawcett mane. They gasp at its softness and its milky colour. They are incredulous, as am I. They say how gorgeous she is. They ask how the hell I keep her clean. I say she has a self-cleaning button and wonder if they can see my gritted teeth.

For we are now deep into one of the wettest, mildest UK winters on record. This, in a word, means MUD. After each of our two daily walks Mabel looks as if she has been on an army assault course: her long blonde locks black and stringy, her legs like dripping clogged sticks, her ears and hound-nose dirt-dunked up to her big brown eyes. If we turn heads on our return journeys it is purely because onlookers are gawping and chuckling at the bedraggled state of a creature clearly not designed to be bedraggled. Think Dolly Parton staggering out of a swamp.

Every day, twice a day, I do what I can with the garden hose, jetting wildly at Mabel's legs while she dances, these days trying to 'eat' the water instead of the hose. Once in the house, there follows the usual kerfuffle with a towel, which achieves less and less as her coat grows ever more luxuriant. (Beware, people buying non-moulting dogs, there's a downside – not a single hair falls out!) Mabel is a thickening hearth rug. It takes hours, literally, for her to dry out. And no, the hairdryer is not an option, because she tries to eat that too, raising the grisly possibility of death by electrocution. Of us both.

I have no option, therefore, but to deploy the laissez-faire tactic of allowing Mabel to dry 'naturally' on her daybed (aka the sofa) on a towel laid on her faux-fur rug. She does not enjoy being sodden. She curls up in a corner, invariably *off* the towel, forlorn as a half-drowned goat, her proverbial crowning glory reduced to a flattened thicket of greyish ringlets. By the time the blonde Afro locks have sprung back into shape (somehow they always do) it is time to embark on our next walk. And so the whole mad mud-wash merry-go-round begins again.

None of this would matter if it weren't for the tangles. Mabel's fur is starting to mat, and getting wet makes it worse. Occasionally, reluctantly, when she is dry and fluffy, I have a go with a brush. Mabel hates it and so do I. She growls, which I find distressing, since upsetting her runs counter to my deepest protective instincts. It also crosses my mind that she might – like that dog of Mum's – burst through some terrible boundary of toleration and decide to bite me. So I hurry through the task, despairing at the obstinate meshing of her hair and reflecting with mounting incredulity on the short neat coats of her Welsh parents. Resentment hovers. This sort of palaver was not part of my doggy plans. The only reason I even possess the brush is because the nice Welsh people chucked one in for free. I don't believe in high-maintenance humans, let alone animals. I have spent my life – decent haircuts and buckets of excellent moisturizer aside – endeavouring not to become too hooked on how I look. I want to age gracefully, ideally with someone at my side, someone who can see beyond my warts.

Diarrhoea Date and I have met again, across a couple of restaurant tables, in a theatre, at a concert hall. Wart-showing is far from our agenda. We are respectful strangers at a dance, circling sedately, making conversation, still lobbing questions at each other like reciprocal interviewees. I nonetheless prepare for these encounters with huge care. I strive to look my very best. I style my hair and make it shine. I dab concealer on the red blotches on my cheeks. I wear my best, most flattering clothes. Part of it is simply vanity, and I feel a twinge of ancient childhood guilt about that. *Vanity, vanity, all is vanity*, Mum would chant if ever she caught me ogling myself for too long in front of a mirror. Her voice was full of teasing but her eyes flashed with maternal warning. We cannot always know

the origins of our beliefs, but I can state with absolute conviction that any healthy awareness I may
possess about the quicksands – the false allure – of
clinging to beauty for its own sake, the insanity of
injecting poison into laughter lines, is all thanks
to her.

But with Diarrhoea Date I know better than to
judge my preening too harshly. The early days of
my meltdown are still vivid, the days of crawling
around in smelly old clothes, pulling the curtains
closed. Self-neglect goes hand in hand with despair.
And my vanity proves I am no longer despairing.

Glamming up to go out is also the putting on
of armour, protection for the muddles and mess
inside. It makes us feel safer. I have no idea where
Diarrhoea Date and I may be heading, other than
to more shared meals and cultural experiences. All I
am certain of is that I must keep my still-wounded
inner self protected. It exploded so badly. It has
taken months to shovel all the entrails back in, for
the tissue to start to grow over. I also have a horrible
new understanding of how heartbreak makes us
even more desperate to be loved, more vulnerable,

more likely to throw ourselves in the wrong direction. With this new wariness I am starting to glimpse other things more clearly too. Like the full seismic effect of the failure of my marriage. How, when it came to new love, I was ripe for the picking.

I invited the man so deep into my innermost landscape. I held the door wide. Warts, warp, weft, I showed him round it all, a willing hostess to a willing guest, pointing out every nuance, every detail. There was nothing I did not want him to see. The trust of doing that alone was life-affirming, electrifying, to feel able to bare so much again to another person. It takes the gambler's spirit to fall in love. You plump for one thing. You pile your counters high. You risk it all.

And still Mabel's luxury coat – her doggy beauty – grows. By seven months the feather curls have evolved into dreadlocks, more like a bleached Rastafarian than a film star's mane, and so striking that I splash out on a photographer son of a friend to come over and take some proper pictures.

I brush Mabel as much as she will allow in preparation, which isn't much, but she still looks glorious. Our professional visitor had been warned of the challenge he would face, the boisterous nature of his subject, but the moment he points his lens in Mabel's direction something extraordinary happens. She poses. She stretches. She stares soulfully into the middle distance. When I say lie down, she lies down. When I say sit, she sits. When I say stay, she stays. In the garden, racing against the rolling approach of thunderous clouds, the miracle continues. She trots, runs, waits, all on command. To say she is enjoying herself would be an understatement. She is a Doggy Diva.

Until, quite suddenly, she decides, in true Diva style, that she has had enough. I issue another command, and instead of complying she simply walks *backwards* – not seen before or since – away from the photographer and me and then turns and legs it into the kitchen. Afterwards, I take her to the park as a reward and encourage her to go completely loopy. The photographs are spectacular. I ponder giving up writing and moving us both to Hollywood.

And still the luscious dreadlocks lengthen and thicken. I decide the Welsh people must have kept back some vital info about her genealogy – a sheepdog aunt, say, or a Pyrenean grandparent. On walks I begin to try to discourage her from splatting in *every* puddle, though in truth I am proud of how she frolics freely, muddily. Thanks to my new training book, she is even coming back again sometimes when I blow my whistle; little wonder since, what with all the fresh meat and fish treats packed into my pockets, I smell like a mobile deli. Other dogs tend to come running too, but hey, no system is perfect.

Back home, the work with the brush gets harder, grumpier on both our parts, more unproductive. One day I realize that there is such a forest of silky white hair sprouting round her eyes that she can barely see out. I toy with the idea of scissors, but don't trust myself. She's such a fidget. And anyway, I DO NOT WANT A HIGH-MAINTENANCE DOG.

But then, one sunny January day, the unthinkable happens. Mabel's poo gets stuck. She squats, her back legs tremble in their endearing way, she's doing her thing, but the exiting poo never hits the ground. There is simply too much hair, too many tangles. Time stands still as I watch her struggle. Slowly, reluctantly, I try the old hoick-up-by-the-tail-and-shake-the-bum trick, but to no avail. I am appalled. I see only one thing: the great matted Mooge reborn. Decades on, an entirely different breed, and I have somehow acquired my mother's dog. A terrible pattern has reasserted itself. Ahead of me lie years of grim procedures with rubber gloves, wet wipes, scissors, the garden hose and a crotchety dog. I could be seventy by the time I get to the end of it. I have bogged up big time. I should have got a dachshund.

The sisters, smug with their easy-care country hounds, think it is hilarious. But I am rattled. I decide to take the drastic measure of giving Mabel a proper bath. I buy dog shampoo and dog conditioner, and stagger upstairs with her wrapped in a towel – no mean feat, since she is heavy, cumbersome and very excited. She licks my face and neck lavishly as we proceed, nearly toppling us both back into the hall.

I tighten my grip, acutely aware of her gangly legs sticking out from the towel at all angles, four muddy trowels skimming my precious recently painted walls. In the bathroom it is waterworld chaos. Mabel, a soaking miserable baby goat, is fast and slippery. She slithers in the bath. She slither-hops her way out of it. The tiled floor is an ice rink. She skids between the loo and the skirting boards. She doesn't look cleaner. I get dirtier. We are both drenched. Somehow we make the return journey downstairs where I fall into a chair, dazed and drained. The drying-out takes seven hours. Afterwards her toleration for the brush is zilch. She bares her teeth. She scampers out of reach. We glare at each other sorrowfully. For by no means the first time in our acquaintance, I realize I need outside help.

Grooming. Oh lord. The very word sends shivers down my spine. For obvious reasons (oh, that power of words to garner layers of meaning) and also for less obvious ones. Mabel is a free spirit and I am going to clip her wings. Literally. I can't tell her how or why, I just have to do it. I am Delilah. She is, not Samson maybe, but certainly a lamb to the slaughter. It is going to cost a stupid amount of money (on that, everyone is agreed) and it will make her profoundly unhappy. A stranger scrubbing her, harnessing her, drying, detangling her rugged hairdo – how can she be anything but traumatized? I fear it might crush her spirit, erase that delectable doggy joy, that priceless trust which has taken half a year to build.

I embark on some serious research, primarily in the form of eyeing up happy-looking, *groomed* pooches and running up to their owners to ask where they got the job done. On one dank damp afternoon I realize, too late to pull out, that the object of my interrogations is the comedian Micky Flanagan. I nearly run away. I don't make a habit of approaching celebrities. I always think how hateful it must be for them to be hassled when all they want is to be left alone. I love Micky Flanagan. His joke about the ketchup in the posh restaurant ('Yes, I'll have the bottle thanks', after being given a mini dollop in a bowl) is one of the very few jokes

I actually remember, because it made me laugh so much. But I don't tell him about that. Indeed, I hold the fact of recognizing him to myself. We talk instead, at length, about the challenge of keeping poodle-cross dogs knot-free and happy. He even, bless him, phones his wife to get the number of the person they use, a lovely woman who comes to their house, he says, to reduce the stress of it for all of them.

I try the number later and leave a message, but the woman never calls back. I don't mind. I feel consoled just to have shared my worries with another person who understands. Being a dog owner puts you in an invisible club. You can confess all sorts of things to each other that non-dog people would scoff at. It makes you feel much less daft. Less alone. Like you do when you read a book that raises all the questions you hadn't dared to ask.

Then Mabel's poo gets stuck again and I dig out the number of a 'salon' that someone had passed on to me because someone had given it to her. Making a booking over the phone, apprehensions surging, I am reminded of the first hunt for a dentist for my sons. You don't want to put them off for life. You don't want them to feel pain. But the job, once in a while, has got to be done.

'A dog grooming *salon*? Really honestly, Mandy,' says my mother, who has taken up residence inside my head as I am discovering dead mothers can do, if you are lucky enough to get through the raw, razored phase of missing them. 'Really honestly' was her stock phrase for expressing total, exasperated despair about any incomprehensible view or decision taken by another person.

I can't do the stuck poo, Mum, I tell her, I just can't.

She has at last taken to popping up in dreams recently too, but always with other people, always on the periphery. They are not the dreams I want. I want to hold her, like in the one that let me hold Dad. I want to feel that tree-trunk solidity of her existence as I did his. I want to be a child in her arms. Even within the dreams I am aware of this yearning for more. She is there, but she never speaks to me, never looks at me. A Jungian therapist would have a field day. In the one that sits with me most vividly we are with a hotchpotch of siblings, nephews and nieces, racing through some snowy Narnia landscape in horse-drawn sleighs (as you do). Bundled up under rugs and blankets, we are escaping from some nameless, shapeless terror. Mum is in the sleigh in front of mine. I am in a lather of fear, but somehow I know that she is calm, and amidst the jumble of my subconscious this comforts me greatly. We take what crumbs we can.

At collection time in the dog salon, it is not Mabel who bounds up to me but a white, bouffant poodle. Shampooed, blow-dried, clipped to within an inch of a neat wiry body I have never seen before, smelling of flowers, head hair sculpted into a fluffy pompom, she is, without any exaggeration, completely unrecognizable. I had asked them to 'go easy', but it is only Mabel's tail, still a feathery fountain, that gives any hint of the dog I dropped off a couple of hours before. Rid of the hairy latticework round her eyes, Mabel's gaze also has a new disarming intensity. I think how nice it must be for her to actually see again, but all I can read in her expression is WTF? I cannot hold her gaze. I am Judas. I am engulfed by remorse. I have lost my delicious dreadlocked Doggy Diva, handed her over to a butcher. A red ribbon in her topknot and we'd be ready for entry into precisely the sort of niche dog-world I despise the most.

The salon owner is thrilled and proud of his handiwork. When I tentatively remind him of the 'go easy' instruction, his face darkens and he takes me to the back room where Mabel's makeover took place. It resembles a sheep-shearing station, fluff everywhere, heaps and heaps of it; not from cutting, he tells me, serious castigation creeping into his tone, but from the terrible tangle of her undercoat and what had to be *brushed out* of her. I must do much more work between appointments, he scolds, like a doctor telling you to cut out the fags or reduce your cholesterol, and incorporate regular brushing and de-matting into my home routine.

I look down at my new trim poodle-pooch, still

rugby-tackling me with joy at our reunion, clearly bearing no ill will towards either me or her stylist, and a penny drops. Clunk, clunk. Her parents, the dapper India and Claude, were not 'short-coated', they were simply well groomed and closely *clipped*. Doh. Did ever a dumber dog-selector walk the earth?

I want to get home and ruffle Mabel back to scruffiness, dig out the Mabel-ness still buried inside this strange new doggy puff-cushion. But at the door of the shop I pause. It has started bucketing. A veritable monsoon. The gutters are already torrents, the pavements fast-filling lakes. My car is parked several streets away. Mabel will be reduced to a wet mat – flattened – in seconds. All that money, all that shampoo, all that smooth untangled fur will be gone. 'We sell macs,' the salon owner announces helpfully, 'easy-fasten Velcro ones. Just to keep the worst off.' I grapple with all my instincts. I am not the sort of dog owner who buys her pet 'clothes'. I AM NOT THE SORT OF DOG OWNER WHO BUYS HER PET 'CLOTHES'.

We leave the shop a few minutes later with Mabel sporting a bright blue 'mac'. In a bag I also have a special, very expensive comb and some special, very expensive spray to help when the dreaded cycle of matting starts again, which the salon man assures me it will the moment she gets drenched or her fur starts to regain some length. I make Mabel hurry, yanking her lead in a vain attempt to steer her round the worst of the puddles. She is getting wet anyway because the blue mac is too large and keeps sliding out of place, exposing her newly shorn body and fluffy knickerbocker legs. Oddly, her poodle head-mop remains impressively resilient to the downpour, bouncing like an ill-fitting wig all the way to the car. Once there, back on her stinky car rug, uncertainty seems to overcome her. She knows she smells wrong. She perches instead of lying down and throws me quizzical glances between sniffing her new strangely fragrant body. I suddenly want to laugh. She looks like a half-sodden drag queen with a tragic backstory. 'It will grow out, sweetie,' I assure her, aware of a pleasing echo of a memory of saying much the same to a sister returning home after a catastrophic perm forty years before.

In the ensuing weeks of continuing diabolical weather, Mabel's wardrobe somehow grows. The blue mac is too big and flimsy, so I purchase a sporty black padded rainproof 'jacket' and also, for walks when it is especially sleety and cold, a scarlet 'onesie' fleece. Scarlet was the only colour they had. She looks quite something, but needs must. Every time I feel sheepish at the bemused, pitying stares of passers-by, I remind myself that putting the onesie in the washing machine is a lot easier than repeating the ordeal of giving Mabel a bath. I might add that such dog 'clothes' are far from cheap. In fact, it would be fair to say, they cost a BOMB, as do the additions that somehow make their way into my arsenal of grooming equipment: mat-zapping brushes, another comb (the one from the salon was useless), more detangle sprays (the one from the salon was useless). The salon man's words, however, were spot on and have certainly hit home.

I introduce a new daily brushing regime and Mabel hates it. She bares her teeth and does her grumble-growl, but I am not afraid of her now. I am getting to know my dog and she is all talk and no trews. I use simple tactics: entrapment (cornering her on the sofa) and treats (to keep her there). And still the mats re-form, daily, just as the salon man said they would. So when, a month later, we meet a lovely girl in a local park who says she has just started her own dog-grooming business and likes to leave her charges looking 'natural', I take her number.

It dawns on me that I have come through a phase of denial. Somehow, thanks to idiocy and sheer ignorance, I have taken on a high maintenance dog. I AM THE OWNER OF A HIGH-MAINTENANCE DOG. As a result, I am now spending more time, effort and money on Mabel's beauty regime than my own. She needs this in order to be kept comfortable, as well as beautiful; to thrive, in other words. It is not the type of dog ownership I had envisaged. But she is already so far from being 'just a dog'. She is Mabel. Her name comes from 'Amabel' which means 'lovable', and a more gentle, joyful, lovable soul it would be hard to find. She is the best of companions. She enriches my life. It is my duty to look after and enrich hers. Mabel's health and beauty in order to ensure my happiness: it seems a piddling price to pay.

9

Chaos Theory

At school I fell out of love with Physics pretty quickly. Things turned sour the day we were divided into pairs and tasked to work out the weight of an oleic acid molecule. The results were strings of incomprehensibly minuscule numbers, all different, but all equally valid (so we were told), and all I could think was (with retrospective apologies to all physicists) WHAT THE FISHCAKES IS THE POINT OF THAT? Learning about things like chaos theory and Schrödinger's cat in later years left me equally cold. I like single, definitive answers. Cats that exist. Round numbers. Certainty. Without that, how can one ever feel safe? Or make solid plans? How can one ever *get* somewhere and

recognize the destination? It was with such con-
victions that I launched myself at adulthood. Take
aim at what you want, and it shall be yours. The
trick is self-conviction. Drive for the line.

Except that, four decades later, the line became a
wall and I hit it hard. I can see now that it was
waiting for me, triggered by a perfect storm not
just of disappointment and loss, but of *reality*.
Divorced, bereaved, jilted, all my self-conviction,
all my black-and-white views of the world, all my
flimsy defences were finally reduced to the rubble
they deserved. In flooded the chaos I had always
feared, forcing me to fully confront at last that
cold harsh truth: that wanting things, even with
all your heart, is not always enough to make them
come true. Mothers die. People you love walk
away. The only certain Happy Endings are in fairy
tales. Potential mayhem lurks beneath the surface
of everything. Objects, people, animals – nothing
stops moving, nothing stays the same. The best
one can hope for is navigation. The instability

itself cannot be conquered. And certainly never ignored.

It would be hard to find a more unstable, ping-ponging bundle of atoms than a puppy. Via Mabel I have invited chaos into my home, and when things are going well I am secretly proud of this. That said, by eight months old she is really beginning to show some signs of successful 'navigation' too. She still performs the ritual of jumping-like-a-lunatic on anyone who walks through the door, but not for very long and only on people she knows. I have put away thoughts of things like rattling cans for good and shout at her instead, which eventually has the desired effect. (The best deterrent is ignoring her altogether, but Mabel sure makes this hard.) Around the house, meanwhile, she has grown so beautifully biddable that it sort of tears at my heart. Whatever I command, she obeys like a lamb. Sit. Lie. Wait. Stay. She has learned so many things! She wants to get them right! She wants to please! Unlike Tiger Lily who, as with all cats (and this is why they too yank on our heartstrings), wants to please only herself. Bedtimes are a breeze – Mabel curls up meekly on her kitchen mat, and each morning I find her still lying there, waiting for our long hello cuddle before she bounds out to relieve herself and bark at the fox scents in the garden.

Out in the wider world now, I feel almost like a 'normal' dog owner. In terms of co-operation Mabel has good days and not so good ones, but then, don't we all. On the lead she likes to go fast, but so do I. We stride along, speed-walkers both. Every so often she will give a firm nudge to the back of my knee with her nose, the same one she does when I am about to give her breakfast or tea. It means, hey, I'm so happy! and it makes me happy too.

Without supervision, however, a rather different narrative is unfolding, one that serves as a reminder, should one need it, that Mabel is in the thick of her teen years. I had been warned about this, the experimenting, the pushing of boundaries. Behind those long-eyelashed chocolate eyes and cute doggy smile there lurks a Mabel Monster, one who, left to her own devices, does not hesitate to go on the rampage, foraging for food and trouble. Not locking the kitchen door when I go out means coming back to find her sauntering down from upstairs (WHERE SHE KNOWS SHE IS FORBIDDEN TO GO) tail wagging, head held just low enough to indicate a sense of her own secret sin. Evidence of the crime is laughably obvious: dirt scuffs on the carpets, doggy imprints on chair cushions, not to mention the contents of all wastepaper baskets – papers, tissues, water bottles – chomped on and scattered across the landing, much like the mess left by foxes after scavenging at a rubbish bin.

Downstairs, if I am ever foolish enough to leave any food container or cupboard open even so much as a millimetre, Mabel sees it as fair game, demonstrating the most astonishing powers of reach on her rangy legs and springy paws. Entire packets of biscuits, whole loaves of bread, multipacks of crisps, cereals, even wads of butter can vanish from the highest cupboards, packaging included. Only Mabel's barrel of a belly and mooching expression tell the full story. Indeed, I would invite anyone doubting the emotional intelligence of a dog to take a long hard look into my hound's face after one of her food binges: it is not the discomfort of indigestion they will see, but remorse fighting with guilty pleasure, interlaced with the glimmer of a hope that no cannon of castigation is about to be fired.

Cannons of castigation most definitely are fired, though I doubt they do any good. I have progressed to being Mabel's keeper, but not her conscience. I am the imposer of limits she feels obliged to obey in my presence purely because I have trained her to. With me there, she won't even sniff at an open food cupboard. As soon as I am out of sight, however, the addict in her reasserts itself, tracing any source of enticing scent and gorging on it. She is a dog, after all, hardwired to respond to the stimuli of smells and physical appetites. My only hope is to get better at keeping the right doors and cupboards closed, managing her instincts rather than pursuing the doomed task of trying to alter them.

The only Mabel crime that continues to make me truly angry is the increasingly rare occasion when, out of sheer devilry or boredom, she decides to charge at Tiger Lily, a bull at a cowering matador, just for the hell of watching my poor not-young puss helter-skelter to safer ground. Mabel faces my cannons then all right, until she is a skulking penitent. Tiger Lily has done so well; she loved our calm monastic life and Mabel has blown it sky high. I will not have her terrorized. On that I shall win.

One day, planning how to manage a new week, it dawns on me that I have grown busy again. Not just because of my new hearty, dog-oriented life, and not just in that I-must-arrange-to-do-things-or-I-will-die-of-aloneness type of busy which will be familiar to every newly dumped, newly divorced, newly bereaved singleton on the planet. No, I genuinely have a lot on. I am getting invited to things: lunches, lectures, dinners, theatres, cinemas. Somehow I seem to have slipped back into being more often *in* the world instead of staring out *at* it. I puzzle over this. I am certain it has something to do with Mabel, that there is some mysterious connection between all the energy my dog has brought into my existence – all Mabel's bouncing atoms – and this new stamina and engagement that seems steadily to have been overtaking me.

And maybe Mabel's doggy optimism is infectious too, because on all fronts I suddenly see nothing but the sprouting of Good Things. At my desk, the creative fiddling has graduated to a thickening wedge of papers, kept in a shiny new purple folder on which I have written the word MABEL in bold black felt-tip capitals. (A new folder is a big event in the life of a writer, and not just because of the stationery fetish.) Even more astonishingly, a potential way to resolve the stasis over Mum's 'discretionary' will has presented itself. It is going to involve a frightening amount of money and a lot of nerve-holding while a house is bought and another sold, but with the right faith in each other it is definitely doable. Such is my conviction, I find myself leading the charge among my siblings to make it happen. At the back of my mind the magical day of boxing and sorting in Sussex shimmers like inspiration, the glimpse of the old bedrock of familial trust and love from which we sprang.

The prospect of ending the lawyers' bills is appealing, but a far greater spur is the eradication of the family tensions that have run on for far too long, demeaning us all. Greed is a terrible master, but so too, it dawns on me, is grief. It warps you. It darkens you. I might have made the most noise by having my meltdown, but I was not the only one to lose her bearings. The death of Mum threw us all overboard. No wonder we have struggled. Without her, we have been reconfiguring who we are as a family, where we all now fit in, how to function with no one at the helm. I start to express such thoughts out loud, startling the siblings. I am 'Small', after all, the youngest girl, the least listened to, the one who, not that long ago, fell flat on her face. Truth be told, I am pretty startled myself.

Mabel might be central to this new phase of positive thinking, but I am aware that Diarrhoea Date is playing a significant role too. He has shown little enthusiasm to meet my dog again (for which I can hardly blame him), but we are in even more regular contact now, and our planned trysts (we are both forward planners) light up the diary. We would not qualify – yet – for Romance of the Century, but the more I get to see of him the more I realize how much I have missed having a man *there,* hovering within the framework of my comings and goings; someone to plan around, to factor in; someone to bounce ideas off; someone to loop arms with as you cross a road. The terms of the engagement almost don't matter. It is simply the sense of balance that 'having someone else' provides. It is steadying. A counterweight. It is what you get used to in a long marriage, regardless of the peaks and troughs, and the loss you feel most acutely when you get divorced. I did not pick up on this at the time. There was too much else going on. Practicalities. Damage limitation. It is only now, looking back over the battle-scarred landscape of the last seven years, that I fully understand the true weight of that countering force, the great space its absence leaves behind. When it is gone you swing freely, but you are at the mercy of the wind.

I am not so much of a fool as to talk in such

terms to Diarrhoea Date himself. We are way off the point of considering each other 'partners', long-term or otherwise, but I start to think such a point is not beyond the realms of possibility. It is the most slow-burn relationship I have ever known, but I start to see that positively too. We are both of a certain age, we have both been through many a hoop, which makes us cautious – and what a sensible and wonderful way to be! This, I decide, is obviously how middle-aged divorced dating should proceed. No more what the exquisite Mrs Patrick Campbell called the 'hurly-burly of the chaise longue', and phew, quite frankly. How could I, of all people, ever again want that I-must-breathe-the-same-air-as-you passion, for which the price of electrifying pleasure is monstrous pain? Uh-uh. No sirree. I am done with that. I have handed in my gambler's chips. Perhaps I have grown up at last. Hoorah!

Mum likes to pop into my head when I am think-ing along such lines. She agrees with me about the chaise longue (she was a big fan of Mrs Patrick Campbell) and thoroughly approves of Diarrhoea

Date's gentlemanly ways. He is just what the doctor ordered, she says. She also says, hang on in there and all will be well. All manner of things will be well. And I believe her.

The first time I saw a dog walker was thirty years ago in Buenos Aires. He was a young man with long bleached hair and muscles bulging under a tight T-shirt and jeans. Tugging on his arms, their leads like parachute strings, was a posse of dogs, big and small, crowding the pavement on their way to hang out in one of the city's many plazas, where there was at least some scrubby grass to sniff, and tree shade from the belting sun under which to shelter. I remember laughing in scornful disbelief at the sight, while rather admiring the brawn of the young man. Dog walking! Of all things! What sort of a career was that? And what sort of people acquired dogs only to farm them out to others for their exercise? I was disdainful, smug in the happy knowledge that such idiocy would never catch on in the UK.

I am not good at spotting trends. Early on in my first career as an advertising account manager, when assigned to work with clients on launching something called a 'personal computer' I privately pooh-poohed their – and my director's – firmly held belief that before too long everyone would have exactly such a machine in their homes as well as their offices. Oh yeah, I nailed that one. And when asked to help in the pitch for a business producing decaffeinated coffee the following year, I was openly amused by the waste of effort. I mean, who on earth – apart from a clutch of nutters – would ever want to drink coffee without its caffeine? I had to give up my advertising career to go and live in South America, but it was little loss to the industry.

I think of the Argentinian with the popping muscles as I start phoning the list of dog walkers kindly provided by my vet. I see it as a business necessity – respite for me so that I can pursue other projects, including getting back to regular writing, and a bit of variety for Mabel. I have no doubt she will love the licence to caper with other dogs and burn off some of her bottomless energy. If I can just find someone nice enough, it will be like dropping a kid at a party.

I quickly learn several things. First, dog walkers in London are in such high demand that most are too busy to take on a new animal. Second, they are therefore (the laws of supply and demand are simple) EXPENSIVE. Third, you might think you are interviewing a dog walker, but it is the other way round.

Surmounting such obstacles, I eventually find a kind, splendid lady, who listens patiently to my paranoid lecture on all the things I want her to take into consideration when walking Mabel, and who isn't put off by Mabel doing her maniac jumping-up act throughout the conversation. She drives off in the London taxi she uses for her business, Mabel packed in the back with all her other charges. I watch from the dining room window as it disappears down the street, nose-pressed to the glass, pale-faced and tight-throated, waving like a loon. The woman has references and contracts and a patently good heart. But this does not quell the terror that I may never see Mabel again. Such is the dumbness of love.

I do see Mabel again, an hour and a half later back in my kitchen (I gave the walker a key). She is a deliriously happy, slithering, gelatinous ball of mud, from her skiddy paws to the tips of her cinnamon eyelashes. Her tail, reduced to a soggy black frond, flings out dirt-blobs with the efficacy of a lawn sprinkler as it wags. I say my thank-yous to the walker and then gently enquire whether she might, next time, pass the hose over Mabel en route to my back door, and better still, perhaps discourage her from total immersion in *all* the deepest potholes to be encountered on local walk routes. The walker is sympathetic and very kind. She agrees Mabel is a sight, but explains patiently that what with the time-slot of the walk and so many other dogs to manage both requests will be hard. I smile and say, no worries, if she can just do what she is able. I enjoyed my hour and a half too much to give up on it. The Mabel-less headspace. My purple folder is thickening. I want more!

A few weeks later, however, I am sending the poor woman emails. Looking back at them now gives me the shivers. It is worse than reading early lame efforts at schoolwork, because there is not the excuse of youth. In fact, it is like reading the words of someone I do not know, someone painfully neurotic and intense, someone patronizing, someone *awful*.

Dear X,

A big request now with Mabel is that if she misbehaves, e.g. does not come when you call, or jumps at strangers, you let her know STRAIGHT AWAY that she has done wrong and put her on the lead (for a few minutes) so that she realizes the consequences of her behaviour are... no fun! Can I also ask that you try not to use the whistle with her, as it seems to be losing its power, and I have ordered another new special dog whistle (!!) which I am going to start to use with some back-to-basics recall training. This will work better if she is not being whistled at in the meantime – i.e. the signal I am going to use with her will be completely 'clean'.

You can tell I have been reading my dog book!! But I have got to try something as I hate worrying all the time that she is going to jump on people or take off.

Many thanks for bearing with me on this...

In response, and not surprisingly, I receive the following:

Dear Amanda,

No problem to do as you have requested but I feel a good route for you would be to use a dog walker who is also a dog trainer, and maybe for Mabel to have individual walks until she is fully obedient. I am happy to do what I can but I don't think I can really provide the service that you are looking for.

Of course I will miss her, she is such a sweetie.

In short, I have been fired. Or rather, Mabel has. Expelled from nursery school. My dog, though sweet, is too naughty to be managed. My heavenly one-and-a-half hour slots of freedom are gone.

I feel as if I have been catapulted back to Square One. The sisters and doggy friends had warned of exactly this sort of stalling and rebellion in the teenage years and I take heart from that. They said it was a hump to be got over, that plain sailing awaits on the other side. I hang on for the delivery of yet another dog whistle and buy lots of fresh chicken.

In low moments, the inherent chaos of a puppy – the never-ending work-in-progress that is Mabel – is harder to savour. Sometimes – occasionally – instead of feeling proud, I curse the recklessness of having made such a life-changing decision when I still wasn't thinking straight. I had lost my compass. I had forgotten how to stand upright, let alone look ahead. I was in a slough of despond and could have stayed there, tucked up safe, listening to pins drop. You know where you are when pins drop. Aloneness may be monotonous, but at least you have no one to worry about but your own sorry self. At least you are in control.

The steady deterioration of my once pristine home feeds such reflections: the mud-crusts on the cushions of the chairs where Mabel is 'forbidden to sit'; the hieroglyphics on the floor from her claws catching during rough-and-tumble games; the grey stains where the biological powder of the early days failed to do its job; the little puddles of brown water where her beard dribbles after her frequent and exuberant visits to her water bowl; the scuffed skirting boards; the smears on the walls; the two dirty soggy towels now in permanent residence on the back of a chair by the radiator, ready to meet the daily challenges of post-walk dousing; the butcher's bones and homemade liver cake taking up half the freezer; the dismembered toys, scattered like body parts round the sitting room; my rapidly diminishing bank balance…

We need low moments. They accentuate the high ones.

Mabel's and my favourite place to hang out is the sofa. She is far too big for my lap these days, which doesn't prevent her attempting to sit on it. We have an enjoyable tussle and then she usually ends up curled next to me, half on the now grotty faux-fur rug which is supposed to be her designated zone and half on my left leg. If I say 'tummy' she flips onto her back to display the special, still least hairy, most sensitive bit of her underbelly, which remains her favourite spot for tickling. She loves a good back rub too, going very still and blinking importantly as I knead my fingers up and down her spine, as if she knows that pleasure like this requires concentration. Sometimes, perhaps because she is bored, perhaps because she is clever, she shuffles upright into a patently awkward imitation of my own vertical sitting position, pressing her back against the cushions, tipping her hairy chin upwards and casting me glances, as if to say, so is this what you do? Have I got it right? Because if so, it's bloody uncomfortable.

I am giving up the fight not to anthropomorphize her. It is proving too irresistible. Another slippery slope among so many. Mabel may be a dog, but there is such a knowingness in her, such a sense of humour, such hopeful energy, only the vocab of human emotions can do it justice. On our hanging-out nights the sofa feels like a small, jolly boat in a hectic sea. Scattered around us are Mabel's most prized possessions: a large squeaky pink pig, a decapitated squirrel toy, a snake without its entrails, half-chewed tennis balls, old marrow bones, gnawed to arrowheads, the hardy string of red plastic sausages owned since day one, and a catnip mouse, tail gone, treasured only because it is supposed to belong to Tiger Lily.

Every so often Mabel will abandon her post at my side and trot over to one of these beloved items and make a big to-do of trying to play with it on her own. She wants me to watch. She wants me to see that playing on your own is a tough ask, that, in an ideal world, she *needs* assistance. If I ignore her she eventually brings the toy to me and sits, waiting, staring at me hard – the sausages or soggy animal legs dangling from her mouth like roadkill. Sometimes I give in. Sometimes I raise my book or newspaper higher to shield myself from the supplication. If I can hold out, she eventually collapses with a sigh of long-suffering defeat. Or, if in a particularly boisterous or optimistic mood, she will try her luck with Tiger Lily, waggling the toy under the cat's contemptuous eye in the vain hope that this will be the longed-for day when her co-companion succumbs to the temptation of embarking on the games of which she dreams. And when that fails, which it always does and always will, she slumps down, toy tucked under chin, and has a snooze.

I whisper 'Good girl' at her then. I want her to know that lying quietly is worthy of my praise. Inwardly I rejoice at her sweetness, at her lack of all the snappyyappy-ness I dreaded, at her capacity, sometimes, simply to chill out, just like the breeders promised.

10

Growing Up

When the eldest was a toddler we were living in Washington DC. Thinking he would enjoy some playtime away from his baby brother, I booked him into a nearby Montessori school. Montessori was all the rage – ideal for small sensitive ones like mine, who enjoyed the calmer entertainments of life – but the place had strict rules, one of which was that the children had to be collected by a teacher from the car, while the parents remained behind the wheel. At the start of the day, therefore, the forecourt was like a drive-through diner, cars entering on one side, engines kept running while charges were extracted from the vehicle, before exits were made on the other side back into the road.

Every morning in the car line, it was, for the teacher prising the eldest off the backseat, like trying to get a limpet off a rock. He howled. He clung on. He didn't want to go. He didn't want me to drive away. I found it desperately hard, but I stuck to my guns. Even writing that now, I feel like a brute. But the head teacher assured me he was fine as soon as I was gone. All he was struggling with was separation anxiety, she said, with just enough of a hint of condescension in her tone to suggest that my parental anxiety was equally to blame. *Separation anxiety.* It was the first time I heard the term, but by no means the last. The eldest continued to struggle, and when a return to the UK a couple of months later meant pulling him out of the place anyway, I was relieved.

Of course you would never guess it now. That son has lived and worked in the most far-flung places. He does not seek out change, but embraces it bravely and with aplomb. So who can say what effect those early car extractions had? Did they plant a fear to be overcome, or did they assist in the overcoming?

★

In my olden pre-meltdown, pre-Mabel days, listening to dog owners discussing the trauma of leaving their hounds somewhere in order to go on holiday did not stir my sympathies. I mean, for heaven's sake, a dog is a dog, right? Find a kennels! Even when Mabel was in her earliest phase of puppy-cuteness, I had no intention of wavering from that view, not once she was grown up, trained and settled. I live alone and my working life is solitary. I need my breaks! And no (since you ask), the compromise notion of getting her a passport and a rabies jab so the two of us can bounce off on joint jolly jaunts across the Channel is no answer. For one thing, prolonged spells in a car and my back would go. For another, only a sadist would take Mabel and her multi-layered luxury coat somewhere hot (for me the best holidays involve heat), or shave her bare, for that matter, in a bid to raise her tolerance levels; Mabel shorn would look oven-ready and I couldn't do it to her. Most importantly, potty though I am about my dog, having her sweet but rambunctious presence on holiday would impede exactly the sort of switch-off relaxation I was looking for.

So when an enticing invitation to go away with friends lands in my lap – for a *proper* holiday in a stinking-hot place, with books and sunbeds and swimming pools and beaches and large gin and tonics and lie-in mornings and slap-up al fresco meals and siestas beneath the shade of rustling palms – I decide it is time to find a decent dog kennels. I picture a firm, friendly, rural place, one that we can return to time and time again, when all those other holiday offers come pouring in; one that will make Mabel's tail wag as soon as we swing into the entrance.

Oh, I know it's going to be hard. I am under no illusions. I know there will be separation anxiety all right – mine, quite apart from hers. Mabel is a dog, not a child (fellow parents will recognize there is a hierarchy of importance here), but I love her. She has entered my bloodstream. The months of ownership and bonding have forced me to come clean about that, to accept it. Love isn't a choice.

Dogs, humans – it makes no difference. Depositing such cherished creatures in institutions takes sangfroid, as I learned at the dodgy drive-through Montessori a quarter of a century ago and have been learning ever since: new playgrounds, first playdates, exam days, airports, halls of residence – that one's offspring get better at fighting down their fears does not make the walking away any easier. Their pain goes underground, but you know it is there. Quick farewells, that is the key. Only one look back. Don't howl until you are out of sight, and preferably earshot.

On the animal front I have two decades of leaving various adored cats in catteries under my belt for the purposes of family holidays. They invariably returned a tad grumpy, and sometimes sporting ear and eye infections, but in a couple of days everything always got straightened out.

Until Tiger Lily, that is. With her, it has to be admitted, my sangfroid has hit a bit of a glitch. Cat feeders have always been the order of the day for her, at absurd and vast expense. But that is because Tiger Lily was damaged goods from the get-go, scooped up off a South London pavement as a kitten, a Special Case. A fact which, ten years on from her rescue, still manifests itself in delightful habits like a propensity to claw even her most beloved humans if startled, to pee *inside* the house when the mood takes her, and a daily appetite for licking the full length of her beautiful freckled leopard tummy until it is an open wound, raw and bleeding. If Tiger Lily were human she would be in therapy. Every week. For life. In a cattery, she would self-combust.

Mabel isn't damaged goods. She remains an innocent. She has no life-dents. No issues. Not yet, anyway. She even got over her neutering op in a matter of hours. Mabel *is* therapy. She is Ms Jump For Joy. Ms Bring It On. Ms 'I Need As Much Action And Entertainment As You Can Possibly Throw At Me NOW, if you please, though I can wait five minutes if you absolutely insist, because although I may be a noodle of a poodle I am also a golden retriever, and one thing we know about is how to relax'.

★

A few weeks remain until the proposed holiday, but my sporadic kennel googling has yet to find any foothold or focus. I am not sure what I am looking for, let alone how to recognize it if I find it. I have bought suntan lotion and stocked up on books. I have put a reserve on some flights. Desperation mounting, I decide to leave the Internet and seek help from my new circle of canine-oriented friends. One personal recommendation is all I need. But to a man/woman they shake their heads. They suck their teeth. They say, diplomatically, that kennels can work well, for the right dog. Or so they have heard. A few horror stories seep out during the course of these conversations, of a traumatized hound coating the back of the car in liquid excrement at the sight of the kennels it was thought to have enjoyed the year before, of a dog rendered voiceless (er... bark-less) from howling non-stop during its incarceration, of another crushed forever to a dim-eyed version of its former self after a stay somewhere that had seemed perfectly fine.

None of my new acquaintances are prepared

to run such risks. Instead they deploy intricate alternative dog-care support systems involving, in various combinations, willing friends, family members, cleaners, professional walkers, neighbours and house-sitters. My spirits plummet. I had a dog walker but she sacked me. I live on my own. My close friends still think I was borderline insane to take on a dog. My neighbours are acquaintances, still charging between school runs and careers. My sons have action-packed working and social lives, as do my siblings. My parents are dead.

I try my new system of seeking counsel from Mum in my head, but for once hear only silence. On reflection, I recall how rarely she and Dad went away once the great Mooge and his successors came on the scene and grimly acknowledge the connection. All those well-intentioned warnings a year ago were one hundred per cent correct. Dogs keep you at home. They are a tie. A bind.

I hold my nerve. I summon to mind a lovely local family who used to boast of sending their delightful, grounded, mild-mannered Labrador, sadly now dead (NB: of old age, not trauma) to a place in Wales every summer for a whole month. It was like a fun doggy boot camp, the mum used to say, with the add-on benefit of the dog returning better behaved than when he went away. The trick, she claimed, was to get the initial visit in early, ideally before a dog's first birthday. Mabel is ten months old. It is the perfect time to take the plunge.

Wales! A fun boot camp! Mabel would be near her first family. Maybe the scents would be familiar, the verdure, the damp... An image skitters across my path, of the likely state of Mabel after a run-around in the lush and damp Welsh countryside with her pack of fellow inmates. Her townie wet-proof gear would be no match for it. There might be some jet-hosing afterwards. A towel-down, if she's lucky. A kennels couldn't be expected to do any more. Her fur would rapidly do its thing, the mats spreading and thickening with the speed of Japanese knotweed. The only viable option would be to get her closely cropped beforehand – not an oven-ready shearing maybe, but a crew cut. Would that be so bad? Helpful, fond memories surface of my sons' insistence on sporting near-shaven heads during their pre-teen football-thug phase, along with the too-big shapeless garments and hateful trailing shoelaces that passed then for youthful sartorial style. If anything it had only endeared them to me more, so plain was the little-boy vulnerability in their bared scalps, the subconscious protection sought by those baggy outfits, hiding the shyness of youngsters not yet comfortable in their own skins.

I hang on to the Wales idea. I remind myself Mabel is NOT a child, she is an *animal* and that I am in danger of becoming exactly the sort of sentimental twit of a dog owner I once (so recently) scorned. I resolve to call the friend who had the nice Labrador, whom I haven't seen for years, and get some details. I pick up the phone and put it down again as the excursions that led to the discovery of Mabel a year ago swim back into focus. The distance. The motorways. The safaris. Without a co-driver I would have to drop her the day before my departure to the hot place and collect her the day after my return. Sixteen nights away instead of fourteen. Sixteen nights away from Mabel.

I glance down at the object of these considerations, stretched out at my feet, touching some part of me with some part of her, as she likes to. She is grinning in her sleep, showing her small tidy white teeth, her face slack with contentment. I reach down to stroke her head and she doesn't even twitch, so used is she to my touch. She has got so big, so long. Her coat is a wavy sea of pearly cream tinged with gold. Thanks to the nice girl we met in the park, it is now kept at a manageable mid-length all over, apart from a dear feathery undercarriage of longer fur on her belly, silky as petticoats, and a touch of bagginess (think Austrian lederhosen, but fluffy) round the upper half of her strong lanky legs. Her head hair is still a frothy mop, and her ears swing so low and with such exuberance that they are a regular hazard when clipping on her collar. Her beard is trim and rust-fringed, tapering neatly under her long jaw, while the hair tufts on the bridge of her nose and forehead are kept in sufficient order to give full rein to her diva eyelashes, rendering the communicative beauty of what they protect impossible to avoid. Adulthood

216

is making Mabel's eyes darker, deeper. Even when she has been asleep they flick open in an instant, tracking my every move, the light in them shifting from mischievous hope to bemusement to resignation, depending on what I am doing. When she is sleepy, or in the mood for loving-kindness, the light softens and intensifies like a dimmer switch. There is no guile in their expression, no agenda, no nothing except what she is.

Wales, as an option, disintegrates before my eyes, a mirage dissolving when you get too near. But the idea of kennels does not. It is my best – my only – bet. I want to go on the holiday. I *deserve* to go on holiday. I decide somewhere closer to home is the answer. Somewhere small and cosy. The opposite of a boot camp. I consult my excellent vet who hands over a list of local boarding options – not recommendations, she reminds me carefully, but places which other clients have found suited their purposes. To my delight, these turn out to be private homes occupied by fellow dog fans, willing and crazy enough to take on a couple of extras from time to time. I start ringing the numbers at once, my hopes soaring. This is exactly what I need. But it is like the dog walkers all over again – excess demand and not enough supply. No one has any spaces. Reluctantly, my eye drops to the final item on the list. It is the website address of a traditional kennels, but it has a fun and friendly name and is only a forty-five-minute drive away.

Slowly I type the name into the search engine. This is the last roll of the dice. I *have* to like what I see. And I do! There is impressive blurb, saying everything one could wish to hear, accompanied by collage after collage of joyful-looking dogs doing cute cheery doggy things. The 'play area' is stocked with equipment worthy of an adventure playground. The sleeping quarters look appealing, clean and compact, more like private dormitories than kennels. I scrutinize every image, every word. I tell myself hundreds of dogs are happy in this place and that I am someone with sangfroid who needs a holiday.

But then my imagination starts to kick in as only it can. I see Mabel, watching me walk away from her and understanding only the absoluteness of my departure. If my separation anxiety is tough, hers, surely, will be off the scale. She has such sensitivity, such intelligence. Even a toddler can be reassured, but not a sad dog. There can be no phone calls, no promises of return. I picture her as night falls and her energy dwindles, wondering why the world she knows and loves has been taken away. I see her sniffing in vain for it round the edges of her tidy cell. I hear her whimpers as she misses her spot on the TV sofa, her yukky kitchen bed, her smeary old dog flap, her love–hate pal, Tiger Lily, and... me. I am her point of reference and I am gone.

I try another look at the fabulous adventure playground but it doesn't help. All I can think of is Mabel doing the haring around she now does if surrounded by too many unknown dogs, when she is panicked rather than happy, when all she wants is someone to step in and help calm her down. Who will know to look out for that? Who will tickle the sweet spot on her tum? Who will make her feel safe?

★

Mum's shopping sprees were legendary and always included the four of us. They took place twice a year at most, entirely spontaneously and invariably in the sales, which meant crowds and mayhem and the buzz, for her, of finding bargains. Her excitement was infectious, and as we got older we learned to take full advantage of it, lobbing things we wanted into her packed shopping basket – action which only added to her pleasure. I went a little mad, she would confess to Dad when he got home from work, her eyes twinkling as the produce of the day was spread out for his approval. And even when money was tight, which it was for many years, Dad's delight was always forthcoming, a delight that had nothing to do with the various items bought for him. He didn't give a fig about those. He just loved to see her, and us, happy.

Of one such shopping trip, almost certainly my very first, I have one of those memories carved so deep onto the hard disk of my brain that it retains the solidity of fact more than feeling. I am three and standing in the heaving sea of a London depart-ment store, a moving mass of legs and shoes and shopping bags. My hand is in my mother's, wrapped tightly, a comfort but also part of a nagging sense of being pulled around at a pace at which I do not want to go. Until, quite suddenly, the hand is gone and I am alone. I turn in a circle, looking. I am certain I shall see a familiar face, but I do not. A slow sick fear creeps over me. My skin prickles. This is the wide world, a hitherto unimagined and unimaginable reality, and I have been left alone inside it.

It was my first stumble from innocence towards experience, the first bursting of that safe baby-bubble into which all fortunate infants are born, part of the maturation that leads to the far more terrible realization (around the age of seven in my case) that death is *real* and one day even your parents will succumb to it, though no amount of such knowledge offers preparation for when they do. Further down the same rocky road lies the discovery of the necessity of sex for procreation, a revelation which, for me, aged just-eleven and a genuine innocent, was almost as shocking as death. Happily, the information came courtesy of a gerbil who squirted pee all over the biology teacher in protest at having its genitals pointed out, allowing hilarity to quickly overlay the fear. I've always been grateful to that gerbil.

My abandonment in the department store that day seemed like forever, but can only have lasted minutes, possibly seconds. Then a set of huge doors swung open and there they all were, gathered in my memory like some sort of sitting for a family portrait. Mum reached out, grabbed my hand, and on we swept, as if nothing had happened. A new unhappiness overtook me then, for not being able to make them understand what I had been through. I was too young. I literally did not have the words. The misery of that was visceral. Maybe that was when even earlier writerly seeds were sown, out of the urge to be heard, to be comprehended; such is the mishmash of what forms us. It was years before I mentioned the incident to the family. Everyone laughed; no one even remembered.

So yeah, Mabel is only a dog, and I deserve a

holiday, but it turns out I am too infused with my own ancient life-dents to risk tossing her sweet doggy innocence at the mercy of a kennels, even if it is one of the best in the land. Instead, I give up. I stop googling, stop asking, stop pushing at doors. There is no solution. Not this year anyway. Which is precisely when (such is the strangeness of life, so wily, so fickle, so surprising) a friend tells me of a friend who, hearing I have acquired a Golden Doodle, has mentioned that she would be interested in 'borrowing' such a dog from time to time, if ever I needed help. It turns out she is part of a family who are 'between dogs', missing a recently deceased beloved old hound, but not yet ready to commit to the whirligig of getting another.

We have a trial meeting, and Mabel, sensing this wonderful woman's readiness to love her, is so instantly and completely smitten that I have to fight down silly snags of envy. As you do when your kids adore a babysitter and you think *So what's wrong with me?* at the same time as recognizing you are an idiot because child-carers who adore your children and vice versa are gold dust and should be rewarded and praised and held on to for all you are worth.

At the handover I am in pieces. They have a big comfy home and Mabel bombs around it with the confidence of one who knows she is welcome. I have brought enough dog luggage for her to move in permanently: an XL bumper bag of food, the tatty faux-fur sofa rug, the yukky kitchen bed, a bulging rucksack of 'favourite toys', her entire wet-proof wardrobe, a stair gate, her cage (just in case), a couple of towels, car blankets, her grooming brushes and comb, shampoo, conditioner, a spare lead, a spare collar, food bowls, poo bags, packets of treats, not to mention a detailed briefing of her daily routines and a vocab list (astonishingly, proud-makingly, long) of command words to which she is likely to respond. I am a joke and I know it. So do the family, but they are kind and dog-loving and so do their best not to let on.

At the point of saying goodbye, I break all my own rules. I hug Mabel (even though she is too bouncy to be interested), and I look back several times, waving and weeping. Oh lord. Once in the car, I let the sobbing have free rein and then take a deep breath. I feel shaky, sad, not yet able to be excited, though I know I will soon. Love is so exhausting, the way it makes us care, the way it opens us up to pain.

Before setting off, I phone the elder sister, needing to confess my pitiful soppiness to someone and knowing she will understand, which she does. As we talk, moving on from dogs to other matters, I am struck by how everything she says, the way in which she says it, reminds me increasingly of Mum. It makes me think how death is a farewell too, and that there is a lot of separation anxiety in how we grieve for someone. It takes time for us to realize that the love itself never goes away, that there is no separation to be anxious about.

On my sunbed I read with the appetite of the starving. A book a day. Fiction, non-fiction, memoirs – reading is such a wondrous smorgasbord of choice, a feast. I gorge myself. I lose myself, a deep relaxation in itself. I feel, more than anything, profoundly lucky that these pleasures are still there for me, that literature can hold no grudges if you half turn your back on it for a while.

Between books, there is good conversation, excellent food and mountains of sleep. I snooze, I swim, I dream relaxing nonsense. I go jogging to the beach, tumbling inexpertly into the sea to cool off. Rested, my brain starts to look back and configure what I have been through with a bolder eye – the meltdown, the recovery, the Golden Doodle – to give it shape. Something fundamental inside me seems to be shifting and settling. I feel newly balanced. I have a man who likes me, I have a family who likes itself, and a dog who makes my heart sing. I also have a fattening purple folder, testimony to my returning confidence not just as a person but as an artist. My only uncertainty is that, while the name on the folder might say 'Mabel', I know full well that you cannot write about a dog without writing about its owner, and that to do so will take courage. A novelist at least has the carapace of her fiction. A memoirist lays herself bare.

★

By the time I land at Gatwick I am busting to see Mabel again. Although I seriously wonder whether, after a five-star stay with her wonderful new second family, she will even bother to raise an eyebrow at my reappearance. She doesn't raise an eyebrow; she goes full-out banana-bonkers. She is Zebedee on speed. She races, she boings, she dives, she hurls herself, she rolls and is generally such a rocket of celebration that tears well again just at the sheer fabulousness of it. I mean, seriously, folks, if you want to know exuberant love, just get a dog. She looks fabulous too, shining-eyed and nourished. I cannot express my gratitude to the family enough. Mabel may have found new friends, but so have I. As we depart, the car boot stuffed with her gear, they gather round to cuddle her and say fond farewells. Any time, they say. *Any time!*

The next day Mabel and I make the journey south to a big family celebration in Sussex – a milestone birthday for one of the sisters. Even more of a milestone is that it is bringing us all back together, round the table at Mum's house, where we congregated for decades and where the brother now lives – the first such mass gathering since the resolution of our troubles. It has been no plain sailing, but here we are, not perfect, but reconfigured. The kaleidoscope has turned.

It helps that the weather chooses the weekend to shake off its grey garb and offer the best that an English summer can provide: a beating blue sky, a heat so still that nothing moves, the air creamy enough to make your head spin. Fat bees buzz at the lavender. The roses stand tall, full blown, ravishing. The Downs slumber in the distance, sleepy purple giants. The hay in the field next to the house, recently cut, gleams a dirty gold.

A group of us dig out flabby old bathing gear from dusty boxes and trek through the field to get to the river, scratching our ankles on the sharp, axed stems, the dogs galloping on ahead. Once on the bank it is a hair-raising, slithery descent into the river, no time for style or preparation. The water is shockingly cold and bloody glorious. We all shriek and splash from the ecstasy of it. Only

Mabel, my waterdog, stays on the bank, a barking maniac, terrified, until a kindly nephew offers to return her to the house.

I am glad. The current is fierce and there is a weir not half a mile away that we used to receive stern warnings about as children. I am doubtful how my skills as a lifeguard, not tested since the age of fourteen, would stand up to the challenge of a flailing Golden Doodle, even one with webbed paws. I don't want to worry about Mabel. I want to soak up every moment for myself. There are so many of us in the water. It is a laugh. It is beautiful. It is healing. We swim, in a gang, upstream, labouring against the current and then float down again on our backs, paddling like big clumsy ducks. My beloved Forster drifts into my mind, a friend, as are all authors who touch us. He knew a thing or two about swimming outdoors, about the absolution only nature can provide. It was he who opened the door to my own knowing.

After saying farewells to my siblings I stop by the local church, picking my way through the gravestones to get to the patch containing Mum and Dad. She is buried on top of him, making me think, always, and with pleasing domestic cosiness, of bunk beds, though I guess she will mulch into him soon enough. *Not Lost But Gone Before*, it says on the headstone, the words she chose when facing the tunnel of existence without him. They were words selected in sorrow, but they resonate with love and were integral to the strength she found to face what has now come to pass. I stand on the lumpy churchyard grass, my hair wet from the river, feeling neither particularly sad nor particularly spiritual, just subsumed by a reassuring sense of rightness, of another circle completed, one of the big ones.

The familiar route to London streaks past as Mabel settles on the backseat, a sleepy angel, all her scatty river barking forgotten. Noting each old landmark, altered by time yet the same, I have a sudden visionary sense of how the layers of our memories build up over the decades, how it is human experience that enriches a place with meaning. The present only derives its shape from what has gone before, good and bad, and what might yet come to pass; every one of our living moments resonates with the oceans of moments that have preceded it and those that are yet to come. There is memory and there is hope. Life, as something lived, takes place in between.

Time is such a slippery beast. We have our yesterdays, but as one goes on they merge more and more with the todays and the tomorrows. Life is not a straight line but an ever widening ring. Nothing is lost. All is harvest. What pushes through, gold in the panner's tin, is Love.

Back home I have a planned FaceTime chat with Diarrhoea Date. I brush my hair. I put on a dab of make-up. I am excited. He has been away somewhere too and I want to hear all about it, as well as sharing with him the specialness of my weekend. He has a big family and understands them. He is also outdoorsy, with an appreciation for things like swimming in rivers. Our screens flicker into life and I start to chatter, as is my wont. And then I stop because I can tell something is wrong. He is pale and unsmiling. In fact he looks ill. I am about to ask if he is feeling all right when he tells me – in the manner of bad news straight, which is the only way bad news should be delivered – that he does not wish to see me anymore. I am not 'the one', he says.

I feel I have been slapped across the face. I feel blindsided. Dumb. I hadn't seen it coming. I tell him all of this and he says he is sorry, while taking care to reiterate that whatever we have been sharing is over. Already I am feeling sorry for him. He is doing a difficult thing and not making a bad fist of it. But I am also feeling sorry for myself. Diarrhoea Date wasn't 'the one' either, but I had still been enjoying our acquaintance. I had dared to feel safe. Dared to feel balanced. Maddeningly, tears are spilling down my cheeks. I apologize. I want, so badly, to retain some vestige of dignity, to manage this situation well. We have been good to each other, Diarrhoea Date and I, good for each other. We deserve a good ending.

I say of course I understand completely, and all of it is fine, but can we still be friends? (Groan.

Platitudes, as ever, barge their way into a crisis.) He, manfully, says yes, though I know at once he doesn't mean it. Truth be told, we have been little more than friends anyway. What he wants is no more obligation to spend time in my company. Life is short and he is busy and I am not 'the one'. The full irony of the situation dawns then: the very thing I valued most, the companionable slow-burn safety of the relationship, is precisely why he wants no more of it. With 'the one', as I know to my cost, there can be no slow burn. With 'the one' you jump right into the sea, off a high cliff, not even bothering to hold your nose.

After the call, which, thanks to noble efforts on both our parts, ends as well as such calls can, I lie on my back on the floor. I am upstairs in my study. The same place where I howled some twenty months before. The same place where I crawled to the window and peered down at the patio, into the abyss. Today I sit up and blow my nose and then go downstairs to make a cup of tea.

Mabel is waiting at the bottom of the stairs, where she always waits. She senses that there has been a change in mood, that something has happened. Instead of bouncing, she follows me quietly into the kitchen, watches while I make my tea, and then comes to sit with me on the sofa. Not on me, but next to me, resting her head on my thigh. She sighs heavily, as if to say, yeah, life can be a bummer, tell me about it.

A part of me is still readying itself for the chasm to open up, the old wound to gape, as wounds do if prodded. I know now, more than I would like, about the well of sadness that sits inside us, the fissures that can lead to drowning. But there is no sign of a fissure, a chasm or anything else, not even when I think back to the man whose desertion helped alert me to their existence. I sigh along with Mabel and sip my tea. I have known heartbreak, and this is not it.

I will need to tell people in due course, the sons, the sisters, close friends. When I am ready. For now I have my dog and my home and even the first stirrings of something like relief. I am on my own, but I do not feel alone. Rejection hurts, but the sense of balance hasn't gone.

11

Opening Doors

Near where I live there is a patch of ancient forest, a green speck of wildness left over from those days of yore when England was an emerald isle, all green and all wild. It is a fortress of oak and beech, big enough to get lost in and threaded through with rough paths, maintained with only the lightest of assistance (by eco-Trojans you never see) purely for the benefit of things like nesting woodpeckers and endangered hedgehogs. A high canopied roof, formed by the branches of the oldest and mightiest of the trees latticing the sky, adds to the sense of containment, of being inside a space old enough to be hallowed. Even when the all-pervasive chattering London parrots are in conversation, it feels like a world within a world, vibrantly alive, pulsing with its own undercurrents of stillness and mystery, of immutability, of all things seen.

Finding wild places to go to is getting harder because they are fewer. It takes work, time, cars, coaches, aeroplanes, money. Wild places matter. They take us out of ourselves while helping us find ourselves. With a shameful disregard for my carbon footprint, I have, over the years, sought out as many such treasures as financial constraints and opportunity would allow, ranging from the Lake District to Patagonia, from Zimbabwe's majestic Eastern Highlands to the jungles of Mexico, from the miracles of Machu Picchu to the steaming rainforests of Borneo. I have been intrepid. I have been lucky. Above all, I have taken care to look towards as many distant horizons as I can, to keep my eyes and heart open to their glories. But sometimes you need to look in front of your nose. Sometimes it takes a Golden Doodle to help you notice a tiny gem at your own back door.

For twenty-five years I drove round this patch of forest, parked near it, never bothered with it.

Even when I got Mabel and realized it might be a place to take her, I hesitated. I was afraid. I have a dispiritingly crap sense of direction (I can and regularly do get lost trying to find my way back from the ladies' in any establishment you care to name). Also, a well-intentioned acquaintance had passed on the helpful information that a dead body had once been found in the forest's undergrowth and that untold numbers of weirdos were known to lurk along its paths. A great spot for walking, she acknowledged gravely, but never on your own.

Isolated places draw isolated people, so this made perfect sense. It fuelled my hesitation. Then curiosity got the better of me and I enlisted the company of a hardy dog-walking friend for Mabel's and my first visit, just so I could see if the place was worth the bother. I knew instantly that it was. Mabel, passionate about both this particular woman and – even more so – about her fun-loving hound, thought I had taken her to heaven. If her shaggy jaw could have dropped it would have. One big hooray of a leg-nudge and she was off, bombing, joshing, burrowing, bounding and foraging the forest's rich earthy troves of smelly goodies alongside her playdate, occasionally boomeranging back to me and the pathway, as if to check that it wasn't all a dream, that we really were somewhere that contained everything she had secretly wanted from life but had never been able to ask.

There was no question of not returning, and yet still I had to muster courage to go alone. The dog-walking friend had helpfully pointed out landmarks like crooked trees and piles of old stones to steer by, but the forest is an odd hourglass shape and I knew I hadn't got the measure of it. I chose the late quiet afternoon of a dry weekday to give it a go, making sure I had my phone, just in case. I kept my ambitions to a minimum, trying to retrace exactly the route the friend had taken, assiduously checking for the wonky trees and ruins on which I had been so sweetly coached. Without her doggy pal, Mabel was more cautious too, delving not quite so deeply into the jungle thickets.

An hour in, however, and trying to get back to

our starting point, I realized I had lost my bearings. Confidence shrivelling, I tried turnings that took me in circles. Every tree, stone and path started to look the same. Sudden noises in the undergrowth began to make me jump. Then Mabel froze at something she had spotted between the trees, her nose and tail aligned like a pointer, growling. Mabel never aligns herself like a pointer. She rarely growls. She barely barks. I squinted, glimpsing a figure among the brambles and broken branches, a hunched old lady, by the look of it, raggedly dressed, hair wiry and dishevelled; she must have had warts on her nose and green talons for fingernails, but the light was failing too fast for me to see them. At Mabel's harrumphing the creature turned and scuttled out of sight. I tried to hurry us along the path, but Mabel had lost her appetite for exploring and was looking forlorn. Deflated. She didn't even want to walk. As ever, dogs, like children, are on to your doubts in an instant; they find you out. She gave me one of her soulful looks instead. You got us into this, it said, now you get us out.

The dusk was deepening, and all my phone said

was, No Service. (Connectivity in the forest is patchy at best, a charming and integral aspect of its separateness – its resistance to the pull of the outside world – but not so charming when you think you might need to make an emergency call.) Panic stops you thinking straight. You feel sick. I was beginning to imagine a night alone among the trees, huddling with Mabel for warmth, when a lone walker suddenly appeared out of the misty light up ahead, a vision. No damsel could have been happier to see a knight charging towards her on a galloping steed, sword raised to slay a slathering beast. It was all I could do not to hurl myself into the man's arms. Luckily I was too busy babbling my need for directions and trying to discourage Mabel – picking up on my mood of celebration – from paw-painting mud slime and fox excrement up and down his trousers.

It turned out we were on the right path after all, just a few yards short of the fork I had been looking for. My young saviour (late twenties at a guess) imparted this information with the minimum of enthusiasm and then hurried on his way, head down. Which gave me pause for thought. He had gone to the woods for some time out, only to be accosted by an over-friendly, faintly hysterical middle-aged woman with a crazed look in her eye and a drip on her nose, asking about a path she was already on, attired in a dirty coat and a lopsided purple pompom hat, swinging a string of red plastic sausages and in the company of a horrible, jumping, stinking dirty powder-puff of a dog over whom she clearly had no control. A weirdo indeed. The crouching witch Mabel and I had glimpsed slipped back into my mind: a woman probably no older than me, out picking mushrooms for an organic bolognese. Yeah, it isn't just the perception of beauty that sits in the beholder's eye.

One of the joys of the forest is that every visit is different. Some days the silence can be ghostly, every twig-snap an explosion, every woodpecker tap a gunshot. On other days you cannot hear yourself think from birdsong, especially if the parrots are partying, or from the creaks and groans of the trees, or the silky swish of swaying leaves, or the squelches under your wellies. Sometimes the rough pathways are bogs, sucking you down, making every step a labour; other times the ground is springy, echoing with the soft thud of each footfall, bouncing you on. In icy weather the great, shifting, leafy roof keeps you warmer; in hot spells it offers cool. When the winds rage, the forest's rafter-branches filter their gales to gusts, and when it's cats and dogs they break up the heaviest stair-rods into sweet fat drips. The place never ceases to surprise me, to make me feel protected, to make me happy.

There is only one tiny patch I do not like, where a path winds past a disused, blocked-up railway tunnel. I would know the place blindfold, since the air there is instantly and markedly chillier, stiller. This is not the over-imaginative novelist in me talking. Mabel feels it too. Each time we take that route I have to coax her past, sometimes with treats because a command on its own won't do. There may be explanations, but a part of me does not want to hear them. The forest lives. I think of it as mine, but it belongs to no one but itself. It has its right to mystery, as do we all.

★

When you live in a foreign country it takes time to get the hang of things. After six months you look back with amusement at your rookie days, glad they are behind you, thinking how in command you have become, knowing some of the lingo, and where the dry cleaner's is, and the cheapest place for petrol; but a year later you realize you had been clueless at six months too, barely beginning, in fact. The same thing occurs a year on from that, and so it continues, a learning curve that never ends, pockmarked by serious dips and peaks and plateaus.

It is dawning on me that the pathway after the end of a long marriage is much the same. Seven years on, and being unmarried is still a new country, with a new language, new systems. Only hindsight reveals the extent of the wrong turns and dead ends, the innumerable ups and downs. There are periods of joy, of plain sailing, of secret dancing behind your curtains, the tingle of certainty that the world is at your fingertips. At other times you slump under the weight of what you have taken on, blank except for the knowledge that you are unequal to the task.

In even the most faltering or dysfunctional relationship there is at least the benefit of having another person to blame. For everything! It can make for grim living, but it is handy. It offers absolution from any personal responsibility for all that is wrong, the perfect route to self-exoneration. Your discontent is the other person's fault. They could 'make you happy', but they choose not to. Hah! No matter that such blame-dumping is not right, not fair and gets you nowhere. (Whisper it, but we are each responsible for our own well-being.) Living alone, there are no loopholes. No hiding places. No cop-outs. You exist in the glare of your own decisions and where they take you.

With a long-term partner, respective preferences can grow close to becoming reflex reactions. You have each taken up positions, about curry, about politics, about music, about whether and how to peel a mushroom, and are past the point of questioning them. If you are not careful you lose touch with what you truly desire. You become entrenched. Every action becomes reactive rather than truly sourced.

A singleton has no such problems. You can please yourself. Yay! You can flirt with the postman, and dye your hair purple. You can binge on box-sets while drinking pints of Malbec and bolting slabs of salted caramel chocolate (in ice-cream or solid form; both are equally good). Except the postman may get the wrong idea and start to harass you, and the purple grows out looking daft, and the binges lead to a sore head and self-loathing and outbreaks of middle-aged acne. Oh yes, the power to please yourself can bring trouble all right. It takes time to learn how to handle it. You may be able to do whatever you like, but you better make damned sure you like what you do.

For over a year after Dad died Mum carried on getting two newspapers, the-one-she-liked and the-one-he-liked, even though he wasn't there to read it. Then she cancelled the-one-she-had-always-liked and just got the-one-he-had-always-liked, poring over it assiduously until her own dying day. Similarly, his preference for eating late at night had driven her mad, but after he was gone she carried on having her supper at the same late hour. She was a tremendous cook, always teasing Dad, especially if the family was gathered for one of her great feasts, for being disinterested in food. If it wasn't for her, she liked to declare, that steely twinkle in her eye, your father would have happily spent forty years living off nothing but sandwiches, eggs and soup. Yet after his death she ate little more than exactly such a diet herself. Alone again after so long, she could not reconnect with her own appetites. His happiness had got too fused with hers. Her sole indulgences were the telly, nibbling sweet things and lying in late, but they never really made her happy, not in that deep private place where it counts.

To say Mabel makes me happy sounds trite. Though of course she does. Just looking at her makes me smile, especially when she is laid out on her 'daybed' (aka the sofa) as she is now, on her back, all four of her big hairy paws floppy and splayed, her tummy fur speckled with mud from her morning walk. She is the picture of not-a-care-in-the-world, the picture of trust, and impossible not to gaze upon without a swelling heart. I also love how much she likes me, the solidity of her body when we say hello or sit close, all that muscle and energy under her mad beautiful fur, and the musty smell of her, and the nudge of her big wet clever hound-nose against my skin, and the Scooby Doo talking noises she makes when she thinks something drastic needs pointing out, like a fox prancing on the lawn, or a mouse under the sofa (Tiger Lily likes to bring them in and then abandon them), or the fact that she really – really – is at the edge of her endurance with the way I am working the hateful comb through her quick-matting curls.

Almost a year into dog ownership, however, it is clear to me that my newfound balance runs far deeper than actually loving the second animal with whom I now share my home. Mabel isn't ballast.

She isn't a partner. She doesn't have political views that sharpen my desire to defend my own. She doesn't care if I peel my mushrooms or mash them to a pulp. She has no notion of how much of a bottle of Malbec disappears down my throat or how fast. She might be a fan of *Blue Planet*, but never complains when I watch *Endeavour* instead, or one of the musical reality TV shows to which I have a serious addiction. I may be fitter and sleeping better because of exercising her, but it is not that either. Nor is it that she is simply and beautifully *there*, easing the burden of solitude while I continue the toil of growing comfortable in my new singleton skin. It is bigger than that. Better. It is something to do with a dog opening avenues that you didn't know existed, inside yourself as well as in the outside world. Mabel softens my heart. She likes forests. She forces conversations. On all sides, for almost a year now, she has been opening doors. All I have had to do is find the courage to walk through them.

★

I didn't realize it was Edmund de Waal at first. I just thought, oh, he looks familiar. As usual, I was too busy focusing on the engagement between our two animals, or, to be more specific, focusing on Mabel, who was throwing herself at his uber-cool big dark hound like a gauche overeager teenager at her first party. It was a blowy day and we were in the biggest of my local parks, both of us dishevelled and dirt-splattered as per. The moment the identity of the other dog owner dawned, there was no question of the play-it-cool stuff I had managed for Micky Flanagan, or indeed for a rather well-known dog-owning news presenter, whom Mabel and I pass regularly on our excursions and with whom I exchange no more than a quick smile and a what-can-you-do shoulder shrug about the weather. No, no, no. This was another league. This was EDMUND DE WAAL. Not just a writer of achingly acute sensibility, blinding intelligence and a forensic ability to encapsulate truth, but the most superb crafter of raw materials, porcelain being prime among them. I mean, those heavenly pots he did, rows and rows of them, feathery thin, glowing like lanterns in their own light... oh my days. He is one of those rarefied beings, not so much an artist as a magician.

Rather as one might expect from one blessed with such heightened abilities and sensibilities, I can report that Edmund de Waal has no appetite for being recognized. As I tussled with Mabel, he studiously avoided my eye, calmly commanding his pet to his side. It obeyed at once, understandably relieved to escape the clutches of my ditzy hound. I got the lead clipped on at last, but found that I could not let the moment go. Despite appearances (Mabel was the one jumping up and down) I was, for once, more excited than my charge. I mean... Edmund de Waal! I had to say *something*. Besides, I reasoned, brain speeding, was I not a fellow author – a wordsmith – as well as a fan? And what harm did praise ever do to a soul? Who gets enough of it? Certainly not me, though admittedly this might bear some connection to the fact that I am not a prize-winning, globally acclaimed literary superstar. On the rare occasion that someone is good enough to mention that they have enjoyed something I have written, I go red in the face and get a wonderful fuzzy feeling in my innards that lasts all day. All month, actually.

E de W is turning away. I open my mouth, but nerves have taken their toll. I cannot even summon the words 'Hare with Amber Eyes' to mind. My brain is a wiped slate. And it turns out my power over language has gone walkabout too. For, with the moment slipping from my grasp, the words that tumble from my mouth are, 'I loved that book, the one you wrote.' Ernie Wise, legendary epitome of literary ineptitude, could have done no better. There is clearly no question of referencing my own affiliations to literature; there isn't time, and besides, based on the evidence available, E de W simply would not believe them. My clumsy sentence produces the solitary benefit of making the great man look at me at last. Just a glance. I think I see bemusement. Or maybe amusement. Or maybe horror. I think there is a half smile. He certainly murmurs something that sounds like a thank you. But then he and his handsome dog are gone, leaving Mabel and me to stare after them longingly, albeit for rather divergent reasons.

★

The friend who helped me choose Mabel, putting the Welsh puppy people through their paces, has invited us to stay with her in the West Country. Wary as ever of a long drive, I decide my confidence now stretches to undertaking the journey by train. It becomes an adventure. With Mabel to manage as well as an overnight bag, I dust off my rucksack from the cellar and cram it with her gear as well as mine. By the time I have finished it weighs a ton, and I have little more than a toothbrush. We walk rather than drive to the station, so Mabel can empty herself thoroughly before we get near a train. I do not want any toilet dramas. Our first destination is Clapham Junction, but from there we have a two-hour stretch to our final stop.

The adventure gets off to a poor start. For the usual mysterious reasons, all local trains to Clapham Junction have been cancelled. Fearful of missing our connection, I take the bold step of deploying my Uber app, only to find – after four attempts – that Uber drivers are not partial to dogs as passengers. I call a local cab company instead, to be told that it will be a twenty-minute wait for a driver prepared to take Mabel as well as me. We miss the Clapham Junction connection by some way. I phone the friend and explain that our arrival will be somewhat later than planned. For some reason I am not remotely stressed, or upset. I have no sense of defeat. Indeed, I feel pepped up. It is an adventure and we will get there in the end. Which we do.

At the friend's house there are horses, other dogs and a delicious hardy little visiting grandson, with chunky thighs and no fear of nose-to-nose hellos with strange ladies and inquisitive Golden Doodles. We picnic in the sunshine, taking it in turns to keep an eye on the animals and to feed and read to the baby, who is so moreish and sweet I would pack him in my rucksack and take him home if I could. Later on that night, after despatching our various charges to their respective beds, we collapse with good food, wine and the energy to set the world to rights, in that effortless way real friends do.

Forty-eight hours later we are hugging our goodbyes on the local station platform. We have sun-burned noses to show for our outdoor pleasures (the scrummy baby was kept safely coated in factor 50) and deeper lines under our eyes from all the late-night chatter. It has been a special visit, one of those too good to put into words, even to each other. Once on the train, however, my spirits falter. The carriage is jam packed, no room for sprawling, for either Mabel or me. It is all we can do to get to my allocated seat. I brace myself for dog-tussles, but Mabel somehow seems to weigh up the situation at once and hunkers down into as tidy a pile as her gangly limbs allow in the space behind my feet, with just her nose and the tips of her paws poking out into the aisle. Every time a passenger walks past, which is often, she draws them in, emitting a sigh when there is room to slump back into position.

I try to do the crossword but suddenly the memory of another train journey is surfacing, rotting flotsam from my meltdown the year before. I cannot believe I had forgotten it. I wish it could have stayed forgotten. On the remembered journey I am

heading to a jazz gig in East London. It is a few
weeks after my implosion. I am only going to
the gig because the ticket was sitting between the
pages of my diary, an acquisition from the already
unimaginable days of being happy, days when the
notion of going, alone, to listen to jazz seemed a
reasonable and fun way to spend an evening. The
ticket has glared at me all day. Like my very first
safari into Wales, it offered a pretext for something
to *do* – the opportunity to feel miserable while in
transit as opposed to sitting still.

It takes a couple of stops to realize I am on the
wrong train. I stumble off at the first chance and
almost head home. But there is nothing to go home
for, and arriving late for a jazz concert hardly matters when you are on your own. At which point the
solitariness of my venture starts to sink in. No one
even knows of the existence of the ticket. No one
knows where I am. Or where I am going. Or when
I shall return. Nothing – *nothing* – I do or decide
matters to anyone but myself.

At the other end there is a long walk to the concert venue, made longer because I cannot find it.

I go up and down the same streets, again and again, unable to locate the address on the ticket. I start to feel lost in a way that goes beyond the geography of Shoreditch. I try the maps app on my phone, but the bobbing blue dot makes no sense; it tells me I have arrived when I clearly have not. It is bitterly cold and I am only wearing a jacket. I huddle against some railings, staring at the ticket clutched in my frozen fingers. I feel a new disconnection, sharp and terrifying, to the person who bought it, the person with enough contentment and confidence to do such a thing. I stare out at the busy street – the world rushing on, rushing past. I have no place in it. I have the strongest sensation of not being known, even to myself. It is like not-existing.

Beside my face a laminated white notice, attached to the railings, is flapping. It is an advertisement for the gig I am trying to find. It has a date on it. I am in exactly the right place but on the wrong night.

With some calamities, you know that one day you will laugh about them. But as I lurch back the way I have come I know I will never find this funny.

All I want to do is to get home, crawl back under my rock, away from the failure that seems to have overtaken me like a disease. Waiting on the platform, I stare at nothing. It takes a while to pick up on the fact that I am being stared at too, quite hard, by a man a few yards away. When the train arrives he boards the same carriage and sits next to me. He strikes up a conversation, as I knew he would. I also know, deep in my bones, that he is not a creep. He is simply alone and sad – his face is a sagging ruin of thwarted hopes – and he has spotted something similar in me. A kindred spirit. We do not wear wedding rings. We are of a certain age. I, too, stink of desolation. When he asks where I live, I lie. I get off at an earlier stop, quickly, so he cannot follow. I run all the way home. I can hardly breathe from sobbing. Tiger Lily takes one look and steers well clear. I slump. I drink a gallon of wine. And still I am dead inside.

My current surroundings swim back into focus. Fellow passengers. The warmth of Mabel under my legs. The crossword on my lap. I start to pop the answers in – ping, ping, ping – I am on fire. Across the aisle I notice a nice-looking man working busily at something in a notebook. He is perhaps ten years older than me, smartly dressed in a dark blue suit and white shirt, with no tie. I am aware that he is aware of me. There is a warmth of some kind, but he does not catch my eye and he looks beautifully easy in his own skin, not remotely the sort to want – or need – to make contact with a strange woman with a peeling red nose, even one blessed with a beautiful dog.

Lots of people have been looking my way anyway because of Mabel. This happens when you travel anywhere on public transport with a dog. A few fearful ones cower and scowl. Most grin and nod. They like Mabel. She allows them to show something of themselves, something we buttoned-up Brits are not naturally predisposed to reveal, which isn't to say it isn't there. Warmth. Connection. Heart. All the stuff we normally keep behind closed doors.

When Clapham Junction finally slides into sight, it is something of a scramble, what with Mabel and the rucksack, and the carriage being like a sardine tin. Most passengers are going on to Waterloo. As we start to edge our way along the aisle the nice-looking man stands up and presses something into my hands. A postcard. He smiles at me. I glance down and see not an email address or phone number, but a drawing of Mabel, a stunningly expert one, in pen and ink, capturing her exact pose and expression of the last two hours, cooped and patient. I am astonished. Elated. Gobsmacked. I also have to get us off the train before it moves on. I call out my thanks, smiling at him through the throng as we move away. I call out that he has made my day. We both wave and smile some more.

Under the picture he has written: *They always say it is a brave man who tries to draw dogs and children.* Not even a signature. True gifts expect nothing in return. They are purely about the pleasure of the giving. They blow you away.

Two train journeys a year and a half apart. Two men. Two versions of me. Memory is our friend and our enemy. It consoles and it tortures. Without it we lose all sense of ourselves, who we are, where we are, where we hope to go. It is our hard drive, our library, our inspiration. It contains things we would rather not recall. But it is only by daring to look back that we can truly see how far we have come.

12

Arriving Somewhere

It is Mabel's First Birthday. The sun shines out of a cloudless sky, a medallion on a cushion of velvet blue. Birds tweet. My owner devotion does not stretch to gifts and celebrations, but inside, a private sense of achievement quietly glows. The day feels like a milestone. A year ago I was a weeping wreck of a pilgrim on Rome's Spanish Steps, loneliness my shadow. Now I have joy in my heart. Now I have Mabel. I took a risk. I got a dog and trained her into a loving and lovable companion. I have stared down my past and I have renewed my hope for the future. Doors have opened. I have walked through them.

The eldest sister is coming to stay. She is soon

to take charge of a new puppy, and as well as the fun of the visit, she wants to borrow some of my equipment. Not all of it, obviously, since the basement pagoda wouldn't fit in her car. In fact the pagoda remains my dirty secret, already plundered in preparation for the sister's visit. I chose carefully, glad to be finding a new home for at least one of the cages, not to mention the blessed bumper pack of puppy pads and a Santa's sack worth of puppy toys. The donkey, christened on the journey back from Wales and these days significantly smaller than Mabel, didn't make the cut. It was a toy Mabel did grow to love fiercely, but she hasn't given it a sniff in months. The reason I keep the donkey is for me. Sentimental hogwash, of course, but it's like that first forgotten teddy, impossible to imagine in the arms of another child.

A birthday treat of sorts for Mabel is that the sister is bringing her old dog with her, sufficiently advanced in years to be behind the reason for the new puppy, but still bouncy enough to be fun. On all our Sussex visits Mabel has been patently adoring of this hound, tagging at her heels like a star-struck fan. So much so that the sister and I have already agreed that, come bedtime, the old dog will go upstairs to join her in the spare room rather than be forced to endure a night of Mabel's attentions. Mabel's love can be pretty hard work if you are not in the mood. Tiger Lily, meanwhile, who knows this better than most, will remove herself and her disgust the moment our guests appear, sitting it out in some warm invisible nook until it is safe to re-emerge.

The visit gets off to a flying start with a grand mucky walk in my beloved woods. Mabel and I may be the townies, but it is good to show that we have some tricks up our sleeves. Both the sister and her dog are gratifyingly impressed. Back home we lie around the kitchen drinking tea and lose ourselves in puppy talk. Passing on my wisdom about crate-training, which the sister has not tried before, makes me feel quite the Old Hand. Mabel has one vice, I boast, and that is greed. We joke about how puppies will eat anything, even things that might kill them, in Mabel's case pebbles, raisins, wads of spat-out chewing gum, and chocolate. I point out all the cupboards I need to keep closed, and the remarkable reach of Mabel's long hound-nose and dextrous paws. And so it continues, through an enjoyable supper, until we retreat to our respective beds. We have one final late-night encounter before turning out our lights, when the sister pops back downstairs to fetch some biscuits she has brought for her dog – a bedtime treat.

I sleep soundly. I do not know trouble is coming. But then that is the nature of trouble. It is an unwanted guest. It offers no clues as to its intention to batter down your doors. Bad things happen on good days, even if those days happen to be milestones that have caused glows of achievement to warm your cockles. Indeed, that is when trouble hits the hardest, because you have dropped your guard, because you have dared to feel that you have arrived on safer ground.

The first hint of anything untoward is the sound of the sister coming up the stairs early the next morning. Very early for a Sunday. I assume that, being a dawn riser, she is retreating to her bed with a cup of tea, but when I peer out of my bedroom to check, there is no mug in her hands and her face is an odd parchment colour. She has trouble speaking. I imagine it is because she is sleepy. Indeed it crosses my mind, briefly, that she might be sleepwalking. But when some coherence finally does take hold, she gabbles, desperate with apology, that she did indeed intend to make tea, but the kitchen is awash with vomit and that this is because Mabel has clearly eaten and thrown up the box of extra-strength painkillers (thirty tablets, a month's supply) which she had thoughtlessly left in a bag on the kitchen chair a couple of feet from Mabel's nose, the very same bag from which she had gone down to retrieve the bedtime biscuits late the night before. She had only brought the painkillers, she explains, just in case her old dog needed one after all the careering around with Mabel. They are the strongest kind, she goes on miserably, sweet-smelling to disguise their medicinal power. She cannot believe she saw fit to leave them on the chair. She is beside herself with regret and self-cursing, and en route to phone her daughter who, as well as being calm and sensible in any crisis you care to mention, happens to be a fully qualified vet.

I race down to the kitchen. I brace myself but am still unprepared for what I find. There are pools of puke everywhere, creamy yellow and faintly frothy, and gleaming with bits of regurgitated foil, since Mabel, in her addict-eagerness to gobble, has consumed all the blister packaging too. Mabel herself is hyper, weird, roaming around. If she could clutch her stomach, groaning, she would. I boot her into the garden for the tonic of fresh air and in case of more throwing up and fumble for my vet's emergency helpline. It is still only eight o'clock on a Sunday morning. I pray for a voice not a machine, and I get one.

The sheer volume of puke has given me hope. I half expect to be told not to worry, that this sort of thing happens all the time, that with greedy young dogs all that matters is the ejection of the substance from their system. Instead I am informed that Mabel's inadvertent overdose could still prove fatal since there is no knowing exactly when she swallowed the tablets (pretty speedily, knowing her powers of scent) and therefore how long they were sloshing around her innards, doing harm. She needs to be put on a drip at once, the emergency vet says, her voice solemn, and even then no positive outcome can be guaranteed since there will be a high risk of irreversible kidney damage, not to mention stomach ulcers, and various other delights which will have to be tested for and monitored during the course of the next few weeks. My hands shake as I take down the address of the emergency treatment centre, thankfully only a few miles away. The sister reappears in the doorway of the kitchen, dressed and ashen-faced, ready to accompany me, the vet niece having said much the same thing.

It is not a happy drive through the empty Sunday morning streets. The sister is in a state of abject unhappiness and mortification, and though I do my best to reassure her, it is hard. Mabel might die, that is the thing. A thing that makes it impossible to concentrate on anything else, let alone offering comfort to the unwitting architect of the catastrophe. Mabel has been very quiet in the car. But when we arrive and she realizes she is being handed over to strangers in a place she does not know, a place of the starkest décor and the scent of chemicals, she starts to weep, volubly. As does her owner. The sister and I trudge back to the car. She is also in bits, but I have even less to offer her now. I know she feels about as bad as it is possible for a sister to feel. I know that it was an accident, something of which I would have been perfectly capable myself late at night in someone else's house, and that given another, less greedy dog, it wouldn't even have been an issue. I also know that Mabel will probably be all right. But then again, she might not. That is Life. There are no certainties. Except those two old chestnuts, taxes and our ultimate demise.

The sister offers to stay with me but I insist she returns home as originally planned. There is nothing she can do. Mabel is to be on a drip for twenty-four hours. Then there will be the tests. One step at a time. The sister sweetly insists on covering the costs for the emergency treatment, which I accept gratefully – the numbers are knee-trembling. Before she leaves we take her dog on a circuit of the small park opposite my house. We make a forlorn trio. Without Mabel, walking makes no sense. I have forgotten that, the space she fills, the power of her companionship. Waving the sister off in her car, all Mabel's puppy gear crowding the rear window, is the lowest of moments, the irony almost too heavy to bear.

Inside, the emptiness of the house is terrible, reminiscent of the old hollowness I thought I had left behind. I swab the kitchen floor and put the toys away. I phone the sons for comfort and then call the emergency vets for an update. Throughout the conversation I can hear Mabel, still wailing. I ask if they can't sedate her, to ease the distress of the drip and of being on her own, but they say this isn't necessary or normal practice and I am too distressed myself to put up a fight.

Aged twenty-five, as the plane took off from Heathrow, cleaving the skies to take me and my new husband on what would end up being a four-year adventure in South America, I can remember, distinctly and powerfully, the sensation of leaving the first chunk of my life well and truly behind. In my young head I had no doubt whatsoever that I was shedding the patchy prologue of my early being and speeding towards the fulfilment of all that I was destined to become. I could sense it sitting on the dazzling horizon, awaiting discovery, the proverbial crock of gold. There was nothing in sight, not yet, but it was getting closer. The moment I clapped eyes on it, I would know.

A little over a year later I signed the contract for the publication of my first novel, *Alice Alone*. The crock had arrived! I *was* something at last. A WRITER. The contract, demanding the submission of a second novel within a year, proved it. As soon as *Alice Alone* was ready for publication, and with the existence of my firstborn a visible swell under my clothes, it was time to return to my desk. I switched on my Amstrad, faithful midwife to my first completed fictional effort. I sipped my coffee. I began to write.

Or rather, words appeared on the screen, but they were dire. Useless. I am a writer, I told myself.

This is what writers do. I battled on, despair flaring daily as the sentences remained terrible and the notion of 'writer's block' slipped from being a cliché into a new ugly reality. It was months before a half decent idea began to form, a shape chiselled out of the granite of my own terror as much as anything else. Eventually, the second novel got written, published, well received. Writing the third was just as hard, as was the fourth, and the fifth...

Name tags are just that. No one ever 'becomes' anything. All that happens, whether as novelists, good citizens, nurses, electricians, actors, doctors, parents, is that we carry on trying to be the thing we have decided we want to be. Effort and failure are integral to the task. We quest. We travel hopefully. There are no arrivals, only crossroads along the way – points of decision – coupled, if you are lucky, with a scattering of those glittering moments that make it all worthwhile: a turquoise glacier cresting a grey Antarctic sea, say; or floating in a baggy swimsuit down a Sussex river; or cupping the head of a safely born child in your palm; or cuddling your nineteen-month-old Golden Doodle after she has made a full and miraculous recovery from an inadvertent drug overdose.

Two weeks on from the drama, and I watch Mabel making tunnels through her first snowdrifts, pausing only to throw me looks of exultant disbelief that such exciting, gorgeous, edible, fun stuff actually exists and that I have only now decided to introduce her to it. Then on she ploughs, golden-doodle-turned-bulldozer, tilling a landscape of snow so white it for once makes her own sumptuous fur covering look a grubby brown. Such are the crocks – the jewels – that light our way; though they can take some patience and not a little digging.

Christmas is a few weeks away and I am going through last year's cards, as I always do, enjoying a last look at the familiar names, the snapshot messages from other lives I care about, before tearing each one in two for deployment in my private recycling system – a drawer of paper scraps to use for scribbling things like deep thoughts and shopping lists. Near the bottom of the card pile I come across one I did not expect to find and which I do not tear up. It is of a cat peeking out of a drift of snow, a cat so identical to Tiger Lily that if the photographer stepped forward to admit my puss had been temporarily kidnapped for the shoot I would believe it. The card is two Christmases old, sent to me by my mother, four weeks before she died. Inside it are the words:

All love darling. Do hope you will be able to start a better year & that all will be sorted very soon. Mum

The once big smooth flourish of her handwriting has shrunk to a line of faltering spiders, edging their way across the page. Her imminent death is in every one of those wiggly lines, although, like so much else, I did not see it at the time. All I saw was the love, which I feel again now, a tsunami. I try to recall what the well-wishing message is referring to and remember a protracted shoulder injury, triggered by a combination of rusty overexertion on a tennis court and an incident while swimming in the wake of a Dubrovnik cruise liner about which the less said the better. I had been through months of cortisone injections and physiotherapy and it was getting me down. Yes, it was the shoulder.

I stare at the card and prepare for the tsunami to deliver sadness, but none arrives. The picture of the cat is spectacular. Mum was good on cards. She had a great stash of them, covering any event that could possibly require human celebration or commiseration, all of them witty or beautiful or both, and always free for dipping into if one was visiting her and got caught short by the need to get something in the post.

Mabel trots over and peers at me over the stack of torn cardboard. She is carrying her current favourite toy in her mouth, very gently, as she carries everything, even bones and carrots before she gets stuck in. The toy is a squeaky ball recently found in the bottom of a bag from the grand clear-out of Mum's things. Mabel locks her chocolate eyes onto mine. Play with me, they say. Pleeeeeease. I take the ball and lob it out of the room and off she skids, tail high and wildly wagging, elated as always to have this particular ball and its squeak brought to life. Watching her, all my affection merges with gladness that Mum's dog had played with the very same toy. It is another circle completed, a titchy one. There are so many. Or, to use some of my favourite words from the mighty Virginia Woolf's *Mrs Dalloway*: *'Absorbing, mysterious, of infinite richness, this life.'*

I place the cat card on my mantelpiece. It can come out next year too. And the one after that. For as long as I want it to. As long as I need.

Memories may be sad, but they are also for feasting on, nourishing rather than nostalgic. Nothing is certain, no. Everything, including love and life, can be snatched away. But that just makes the cherishing all the sweeter.

The hardest part of writing a novel is the ending. You want to round things off, to bring a sense of satisfaction, but if you are not careful the clank of contrivance can ruin things. Your tale should feel credible – 'real' – yet even the fact of having a conclusion is the biggest artifice of all. The narratives of our own lives have no neatly tied end points, not until the obvious one anyway, and even that can be a hell of a mess. Fiction can mirror, echo, imitate, enhance, but in the end a novelist needs some trickery to seal the deal.

This is not a novel. So no trickery has been called for, other than holding fast to the most sincere intention of writing nothing that might cause upset to others. We cannot speak for those around us anyway. We cannot presume to say what they feel. Ever. We are each the protagonists of our own stories and can only speak for ourselves. Even so, this is not a book I could have envisaged writing until it came into being. It originated as the desire to formulate thoughts about the acquisition of a heart-melting puppy, but then grew, organically and inevitably, into the zigzagging story of the travails of the puppy's owner instead.

Mabel is only a dog, but she has helped me have faith in the world again. Just being around her boosts my oxytocin and serotonin levels. She makes me feel lucky again. She gives me pleasure – every day – from the way she looks, the things she does. She has unearthed the child in me, not just the earnest ten-year-old I had forgotten about, composer of ardent prayers for canines and suffused with a longing to possess a hound of her own, but the girl who is still very much in existence, the one who likes charging around outside getting fresh air, wind blasting her hair, mud splattering her wellies.

I am by no means sure I will ever get another dog. Life is the proverbial journey, and it feels like pure good fortune to have stumbled upon Mabel to travel this bit of the stretch with me. She was a project for a middle-aged optimist who had lost her optimism, a writer who couldn't write, a daughter who had lost her mum, a lover who had lost her love. She was Something To Do and still is, every day. She demands effort and commitment. She has her off days and her moments of inspiration. She is a work-in-progress, as are we all.

It was perhaps cheesy and obvious to decide, peering into the abyss a year ago, that a puppy might put a smile back on my face. What I had no inkling of was the depth of the restorative effect in store nor the true nature of what I was in fact trying to overcome. For while heartbreak and bereavement may have been the trigger for my felling, it has grown ever clearer to me that I was already in freefall and did not know it. I had grown up instilled with a perfect paradigm for marriage and family, but failed to make it work. For several years I had blundered on from that failure, keeping busy, not acknowledging the toll it had taken, how thin my skin had become. The words pride and fall come to mind.

It has been a year of reshaping, reconfiguring, restoring. A year of discovering there are other paradigms that work. A year of learning how to love those who have gone. I became the owner of Mabel. I had no idea it would lead to taking ownership of myself.

Acknowledgements

A huge thanks to Amanda Ridout for suggesting that I write about my dog (and me), and for all the encouragement she gave as *For The Love of a Dog* came into being.

Special thanks to my most near and dear, for all their support and comfort when it was sorely needed, above all, my beautiful sons, Ben and Ali; my sisters and brother, Jane, Fi and Ed; my friends, Gilly H, Gilly O, Melanie W, Celia R, Fi & Andrew H-C and the many others who listened and stood by.

I want to offer a heartfelt thank-you to the whole team at Head of Zeus, especially my editor, Ellen Parnavelas, for the wisdom of her input and her unbridled enthusiasm, not just for her new author, but for her new author's dog. I also remain constantly grateful to my wonderful techy expert, Christian Allen, for keeping my various online platforms working efficiently and looking far more up-to-date than their owner warrants.

And to all my many Mabel helpers over the last two years – Gilly Oakley, Jane Ball, Ciaran & Sue Moore, Amanda & Carmela Shiberass, Ruth Naibagkar, Michelle & Ashleigh Benson, Stephanie Fearon, Gary & Sao Matos – my gratitude knows no bounds. *For The Love of a Dog* would have taken twice the time without your assistance. Mabel may have made brilliant friends, but so have I.

Final thanks must go to my unwittingly glorious and gorgeous Golden Doodle, for her big heart and her gentleness, and for being a woman's best friend.